THE
PrEP
DIARIES

A SAFE(R) SEX MEMOIR
EVAN J. PETERSON

LETHE PRESS
MAPLE SHADE, NEW JERSEY

Published by Lethe Press
118 Heritage Ave, Maple Shade, NJ 08052
lethepressbooks.com

Cover and interior design by Inkspiral Design
Author photo (front cover) by Siege Lehman

*For everyone who has survived the
AIDS crisis, but especially for all
of those who haven't, and for the
generation coming in.*

1
PROLOGUE: Once Upon A Time in Miami...

5
ONE: What Do You Get Into?

21
TWO: How I Lost My Virginity in the Age of HIV

45
THREE: Still Losing My Virginity Over Here

57
FOUR: Love and Butt Stuff

63
FIVE: Interlude (In a World...)

67
SIX: Super Power: Undetectable

85
SEVEN: Interlude (Waking Up)

91
EIGHT: How I Learned to PrEP

107
NINE: Unpacking the Fudge:
An Exploration of Anal Sex, Condoms and Shame

123
TEN: #TruvadaWhore

143
ELEVEN: Sage Your Asshole and Auld Lang Syne

151
The PrEPilogue

EVAN J. PETERSON

Prologue
Once Upon A Time In Miami...

30 tablets

℞ only

TONY OPENED THE bottle of Sprite and took a great and frothing gulp from it. He passed it to Tyler. The Florida heat swallowed the pavement, the trees, the broken bits of glass across the concrete, the four boys and their bicycles. The suburban Miami air smelled of fresh and caustic tarmac and melaleuca.

Tyler looked at the plastic bottle. "I don't think we should share. What if someone's sick?" Tyler's younger brother, Bryce, fiddled with the brakes on his bicycle. We all stood still in the shade taking a break from urban adventuring.

Tony, ever the coercive Tom Sawyer, belched and said, "Why? I don't gots AIDS. Evan don't gots AIDS."

I can't remember if Tyler drank from the bottle. I know I did, though I hated soda. Tony could convince me to do many things I'd refuse from anyone else. He once got another boy to prank-call his girlfriend and pretend to be a male stripper. He was an unusually erotic child—even in a sleazy place like Miami in the '90s.

We started receiving sex education in fourth grade. This was to prevent pregnancies and STIs. This was to teach children how to avoid becoming victims of pedophiles. I recall having little workbooks to color, the children in the illustrations plump and large-headed, their eyes merely vertical lines. I remember an illustration of a boy and a girl at the beach, their swimsuits labeled "Privates," with the caption that these are the places where it's not okay for adults to touch children.

I'm not sure how old I am in the memory with Tony and those brothers. I don't recall ever seeing the brothers again. I couldn't have been all that old, because this is my earliest memory of hearing someone talk about AIDS. I'd probably heard the word before, snatched from the air of grown-up conversations, much like I'd snatched out the word "homosexual" and needed to know what that meant. Perhaps I was nine and the year was 1991. If I didn't really know what AIDS was, I must not have gone through the sex unit in fourth grade.

I was born in early 1982. This means that I have lived my entire life in a world in which AIDS and subsequently HIV are public topics.

According to the usually accurate Wikipedia, "In the general press, the term GRID, which stood for gay-related immune deficiency, had been coined. The CDC, in search of a name, and looking at the infected communities, coined 'the 4H disease,' as it seemed to single out homosexuals, heroin users, hemophiliacs, and Haitians. [*Author's note: the fuck is that all about?*] However, after determining that AIDS was not isolated to the gay community, it was realized that the term GRID was misleading and AIDS was introduced at a meeting in July 1982. By September 1982 the CDC started using the name AIDS."

The miserable, vapid Madison Montgomery, a character played by Emma Roberts on season three of *American Horror Story*, puts it this way: "I am a millennial. Generation Y; born between the birth of AIDS and 9/11, give or take."

AIDS and I were named the same year. Evan Joseph Peterson. Acquired Immune Deficiency Syndrome. I guess that makes me the perfect millennial—I graduated high school in the year 2000, to much fanfare and absolutely no disasters. The doomsayers were a year off.

If we consider the day AIDS received its name to be its "birthday," AIDS shares a July 27 birthday with the philosopher and culture critic Jean Baudrillard, *Dungeons & Dragons* co-creator Gary Gygax, actors Maya Rudolph and Jonathan Rhys Meyers, and baseball player Alex Rodriguez. The Geneva

Convention was signed on this date in 1929. In 1996, when I was fourteen, the Olympics were bombed in Atlanta, Georgia.

One year prior to AIDS's birthday, on July 27, 1981, six-year-old Adam Walsh was kidnapped in Hollywood, Florida, very near where I grew up and where my parents now live. Adam's head was found two weeks later. The rest of him was never recovered. His father, John Walsh, went on to create and host *America's Most Wanted*. That's the world into which I was born.

HIV was later named, in 1986. I was four years old. I've never known a world without AIDS, although I never witnessed someone dying from it firsthand. By the time I was old enough to have HIV-positive friends, people were no longer crumbling like desiccated orchids at every turn.

Instead, I came of age in the latter half of the '90s and achieved legal adulthood two months into the twenty-first century. By the time I came out and began going to gay bars and gay-owned businesses, the biggest breakthroughs in HIV treatment were the new drug cocktails, touted to bring people from their very deathbed back to thriving life, the men in gay periodicals sporting tattoos of biohazard symbols and pecs like coconuts.

Headline: *I Was on My Deathbed, and Now Look at Me.*

This was my childhood and adolescence. For me, GRID, AIDS, and HIV were not varying names for a sneak-attack plague that wiped out half the homosexuals in a neighborhood. I was too young to know HIV on those terms. To me, it was a vague plague, unspecific, something waiting in the shadows like a pedophile. It festered on the tips of needles lying in the gutters along Hallandale Beach Boulevard and Greynolds Park, or strategically placed in pay-phone coin returns or movie theater seats, if you believed the urban legends. We told one another at school, "Don't check the phones for quarters in the slot. People put dirty needles in there, and then when you prick your finger, the phone rings and the voice on the other end says, 'Welcome to the world of AIDS.'"

Aside from this strange hybrid of *Sleeping Beauty* and *The Ring*, I had little to fear from HIV—until I realized I was attracted to other boys. I remember seeing picket signs creating an acronym from GAY: "Got AIDS Yet?" and other ones that read, "Homosexuality is the disease. AIDS is the cure." Because only gay people contract HIV. Especially those lesbians.

But you know what? Enough with that. This isn't a book about a plague. You've likely read that book. Several of those books. You've probably watched *Philadelphia* and *The Normal Heart* and *RENT*, and I certainly hope you've seen *Jeffrey*. Those aren't my stories. I've never known someone who died of AIDS-related complications, and I now have many HIV-positive friends who lived through the AIDS crisis in the '80s and '90s.

This book is a time capsule marking an era on Earth, not just America, when we finally—finally!—have a medicine that prevents the transmission of HIV, and prevents it so remarkably well that out of tens of thousands of people in North America alone using it, there have been only three reported cases of people who took Truvada every day and contracted HIV anyway. And yet people still resist PrEP.

This is a book about the conversations happening on Facebook and apps like Grindr and Scruff (where I first learned about PrEP). This is a book about new conversations, often just as awkward, happening in bedrooms and at bars, the language of romance and casual sex, the semiotics of getting off.

It's about HIV-positive people in relationships with HIV-negative people, none of them worried about the virus. It's about the privilege of healthy promiscuity, arguably a human right, without worrying that we're going to wither away any day now as a result of our actions.

This is a book about how PrEP is changing our world, leading us to redefine what "safe sex" even means anymore.

This is a book about the end of the twentieth century and the dawn of the twenty-first, in which we will finally defeat AIDS and make it more than a footnote in history, but history nonetheless. AIDS will be talked about like the Bubonic Plague. Perhaps the AIDS crisis will be talked about as a historical period in which the lives of queers and poor people and people of color could've been saved, but instead they were left to die. We died too quickly to count us, so we made a quilt that stretches for literal miles to say, "These are the names of people who lived and died and they matter. I matter too."

Most of all, this is a book about sex, hope, relationships, and the future.

EVAN J. PETERSON

One

What Do You
Get Into?

30 tablets

R only

THE PILLS ARE sky blue. Large, but not horse pills. The corporate stamp, GILEAD, is printed on them just like that, all caps, the pharmaceutical equivalent of a copyright insignia. This is Truvada, prescribed for a decade and a half to suppress HIV infections. Now, as PrEP, it has been prescribed to HIV-negative people since 2012 to prevent HIV infections.

PrEP is highly effective. In study after study, the pills had at least a 99% effectiveness rate when taken daily and combined with other forms of prevention (the usual: using condoms and knowing a partner's HIV status, including the highly *non*contagious poz-undetectable).

PrEP stands for "Pre-Exposure Prophylaxis." In layperson's terms, that means you take it before you're exposed to HIV and it blocks the virus. The drug has been around for a decade as an integral part of PEP, "Post-Exposure Prophylaxis," available for a limited course to those who believe they've likely been exposed to HIV, a sort of morning-after pill for the virus. In fact, the discussion of this breakthrough is startlingly similar to the one around the birth control pill, which we've capitalized and iconized into simply the Pill.

People are still agonizing over the Pill. Politicians and pundits are still shaming women for using it, saying that the Affordable Care Act shouldn't cover it, saying no one's taxes should have to cover someone else's promiscuity. In its early days, the conversation was even more hateful and vitriolic than it is now. Women were called "whores" and worse for merely *wanting*, let alone using, a pill that would allow them to have control over their own pregnancy. This hatred runs deep. Remember when Phyllis Schlafly claimed that "sexual harassment on the job is not a problem for virtuous women"? Wowsers.

There are more parallels than this between PrEP and the Pill. Each one only prevents one particular condition, leaving an opening for critics to claim that each medication leads to the spread of STIs. Also, neither is foolproof, though the current laboratory research shows that Truvada is even more effective than birth control pills at preventing what it's intended to prevent. Both medicines are nonetheless attacked for their reliability. Of course, the Pill has the added factor that when it doesn't work, a woman's next recourse is an abortion.

It's bizarre, not to mention deeply insulting to homosexuals, that some folks continually discuss homosexuality and abortion in the same sentence. This is beyond sex shame; for pro-life advocates, it's literally comparing the killing of a baby to having sexual relationships and getting married. Anything that disrupts the "natural" order and the narrowest definition of "family." Imagine the things they'd say about PrEP.

Wait—I don't have to imagine. The weirdest part of the PrEP conversation over the last few years has been the sex shame directed at gays by other gays. Just like women shaming each other for using the Pill and wanting to enjoy sex without pregnancy, I've seen countless gay men direct vicious verbal attacks at one another for wanting to enjoy condomless sex without a risk of HIV.

This is really happening. That's how conditioned we are to think that only condoms will save us, that promiscuity is one of the gay community's gravest sins. I'd say our oft-ridiculous clothing choices are far worse than casual sex, with more collateral damage to the community image.

On second thought, the Truvada pills aren't quite sky blue, but more Smurf-blue, unassumingly candy-like and cartoonish, like pills you see psych ward patients taking in movies. Pretty nonthreatening for something rumored to soften my bones, damage my liver, and transform me *Reefer Madness*-style into a sex-addicted orgy queen.

It took me several months to get the pills—for free, care of insurance and Washington State's drug-assistance program—into my hands, and there was something unreal about finally holding the "miracle" HIV-prevention pill.

I had my *Matrix* moment, except that this blue pill didn't send me back into a fantasy created by our mechanical overlords. This blue pill promised to unlock new possibilities of intimacy, not just sex but mental confidence and emotional connections. Like Miss Keanu, I shrugged my dainty shoulders and swallowed. The pill was slightly sweet.

Then I shit four times in three hours. I'm just reporting facts here. Nonetheless, I didn't suffer stomach cramps, like some people do. I just felt a little funny inside, a little bit off, and I had to use the bathroom several times. Then I was fine. I had no further stomach issues after those first few hours. I used to suffer from several digestive issues, and if anything Truvada has actually helped regulate one or two of them. I was worried that Truvada would be tough on my system, but I've had no negative side effects. Pooping four times in a row was just a fluke. I even felt well enough to go on a date to the beach that evening, but sadly, we didn't make out. Levi, if you're reading this, we can still do that, and I don't need my towel back.

I started taking PrEP because I was still afraid of AIDS. At thirty-two years old, I was sick and tired of that. I was sick and tired of *being* sick and tired, to quote civil rights leader Fannie Lou Hamer. I had been hooking up with Kent, who is HIV-positive. Before Kent, I dated Nick, who is also HIV-positive. In my early thirties, I was meeting a lot of sexy, kind, interesting, intelligent poz guys, and I had run out of reasons not to date them.

Even so, here's something many people still don't get: PrEP is often redundant in serodiscordant relationships if the poz partner is undetectable. The plea to make PrEP available for such couples ignores this, and it perpetuates ignorance about the reality of the undetectable status. I got on PrEP even though I was having sex with poz-undetectable guys because I wanted one more layer of protection, but I also hadn't had a boyfriend in several years. Those of us who aren't blessed with steady relationships need PrEP more than those who are.

Certainly, sex can be predictable and easy to plan in and even out of a relationship, but what about when we surprise ourselves? An unexpected encounter with a still-affectionate ex-lover? A brief sign-on to Tinder or Scruff, just to see who's around?

For heaven's sake, what about Halloween?

I've had a great time with no physical side effects. I have access to a simple pill that I take every day, and it's remarkably effective against my contracting HIV, the single greatest plague of my lifetime. Add to that the use of condoms and knowing your partners' HIV status for certain as negative or poz-undetectable, and transmission becomes virtually impossible—"virtually," in this case, meaning that transmission is so incredibly unlikely that we can reasonably call it 100% protection. "Virtually impossible" doesn't mean "close to impossible" or "next door to impossible" or "lives across the street from impossible." It means, "Stop your damn worrying and relax, because the chances of you contracting HIV under these circumstances are microscopic, okay?"

Is this so difficult to believe? It is. I had difficulty accepting it at first. It's not that my rational mind found it illogical. It's that my superstitious mind found it contradictory to everything I'd known my whole life. Truvada did feel like science fiction. We've had an HIV vaccine dangled just out of reach for a decade or more. We've been told that the HIV retrovirus is incredibly challenging to fight with pills, and that it mutates quickly. PrEP isn't science fiction, though; it's the future of HIV prevention.

I have lived my entire life in a world in which HIV has been a public concern, just as my nephews have lived theirs in a world of home computers and the internet, which I didn't have until I was thirteen. They don't truly understand life without these things, as I don't understand a pre-HIV queer community.

My children (when I have some) will live entire lives in a world in which augmented reality technology is a daily convenience. They—we—will look at any sign in a window, and through our glasses we will be given options such as opening a drink menu, reading the history of a landmark building, or taking a virtual tour of the premises. We will walk past a movie poster and have the option to see a trailer for the film in that very moment.

For now, I am living in the future foretold by countless science fiction writers.

My dog has a tiny computer chip under his skin that will allow me to locate him if he ever runs away. My godmother, a diabetic former cyborg, has three kidneys and two pancreases. There was no reason to remove the old when transplanting the new. She used to have a computer on her hip that plugged directly into her body, feeding her insulin.

I have a device in my pocket that acts as a video telephone, an encyclopedia of all human knowledge, and a match-making catalogue to pick out nearby compatible sex partners. I feel like Barbarella. This is the future which tantalized us when we were kids, and PrEP is part of that for my generation.

My entire life I've been warned, cautioned, and begged to practice "safe" sex. I was conditioned, *1984* style, to be a devout believer that sex could kill me. As a gay guy, that belief was reinforced tenfold and every day. No one could convince me otherwise. Luckily, I was often taught how to practice safe sex correctly. Soon, we began calling it "safer" sex in order to include the margin of error. Hand-wringers came up with a slogan for kids and queers: "The safest sex is abstinence"—except that abstinence is the opposite of sex. "The safest way to exercise is not to exercise!" Now I sound like George Carlin.

To say "the safest sex is abstinence" is as foolish as saying the best way to avoid a car accident is not to leave the house. Don't even walk around outside—a drunk driver might jump the curb and crush you against a tree. Then again, you are far more likely to pet a cute dog, buy delicious treats from a street vendor, make a friend, or get laid. I risk the minute chance of getting hit by a car for all of those. Most days, I just want to pet the cute dogs.

We have to face the fact that the emphasis on abstinence has done little or nothing to prevent the spread of STIs and unplanned pregnancies. Sex education is health education, which is science education. Without even getting into the religion discussion, it has become clear that abstinence education simply doesn't work. It's not healthy. People, regardless of their attractions, are going to fuck. A lot of them are going to fuck without condoms, either because they didn't learn how and why to use them, or because they simply don't like condoms.

There are other social issues in play as well. In the United States, rates of HIV infection are significantly higher among Blacks and Latinos than Whites in general (regardless of gender and sexual orientation). The mix of systemic classism and racism has led to less access to prevention resources for Latino Americans and African Americans. That's not an accusation, an excuse, or a liberal pity party. That's simply what is happening.

This brings us to the topic of access. In the U.S., we're still working out the social impact of the Affordable Care Act (which, as of the latest edit of this book, will likely be demolished by the Trump administration). The blessing of many insurance providers is that they'll pay for PrEP, which on its own would be over one thousand dollars a month. In America, unless you're quite wealthy, you need insurance to afford medical care. I certainly need it. One reason PrEP hasn't caught on around the world is the cost, and I do understand that. I don't want to make Truvada sound like it's a perfect miracle that is given to any soul in need.

Nonetheless, there are drug-assistance programs (DAPs) popping up around the U.S. to help people pay for the medicine. Gilead Sciences will also supplement the cost for qualifying applicants. In the state of Washington, where I live, the Affordable Care Act has made it possible to move health department funding around. Federal money that was going toward making sure HIV-positive people had the medicines they need is now being put toward supplying PrEP to those who need the cost covered. That's been one big blessing of Obamacare/ACA. David A. Kern, former manager of the Infectious Disease Prevention Section of the Washington State Health Department, teamed up with Richard Aleshire of the state's HIV Client Services Program to bring PrEP coverage to Washington State. This happened within the Department of Health at the program level, without bringing the politicians into it. The funding is there (for now) and it's being used to prevent new HIV infections. The state DAP is of course available to all those who qualify, regardless of gender and sexual orientation. Another factor making this all possible is the fact that Washington has state funding for HIV prevention, whereas most states only have federal funding. Our state's PrEP DAP has been an unusual thing, unfortunately.

It's important to remember that neither Gilead's drug assistance nor Washington's covers the doctor visits and labs necessary to continue a PrEP prescription. Those on a preventative Truvada regimen are required to have multiple blood tests every three months. Some people who need PrEP can't afford that.

For now, let's set race and economic issues aside. These are very important to understand in the fight against HIV, but they're part of a bigger picture of what has and has not worked to eradicate HIV so far. We can't treat HIV as a gay thing or a race thing or a poverty thing, precisely because people have sex across racial, sexual, and economic divides. Just as sex happens between Black and White and Latino and Middle Eastern and Asian partners, straight people sometimes have sex with gay people, and bisexual people exist in large numbers. In fact, there are more straight- and gay-identifying people who are bisexual in practice than most people assume. Sex happens. Sex transcends identity.

The irrational logic that people will only have sex with their own kind isn't just bigoted; it's what led to the pandemic in the first place—thinking that HIV was going to only affect gays or drug addicts, as though everyone who likes the same sex is 100% homosexual in practice, and straight people are 100% heterosexual. As though drug addicts always look like drug addicts (whatever that means), and "normal" people don't have sex with them. As though queers and drug addicts weren't worth protecting.

It's like the Edgar Allen Poe story "The Masque of the Red Death": those in power shut themselves up in a castle, while outside the commoners are dying in droves from a plague.

Spoiler: the plague gets into the castle anyway.

WHEN I STARTED my freshman year of Florida State University in August of the year 2000, we had a few days of freshman orientation. We were split into groups to tour the campus and receive a quick rundown of student resources. At one point, we had a group activity involving color-coded rubber bands. I don't recall exactly what we were asked to do, but it involved introducing ourselves to one another, shaking hands, and collecting rubber bands. I could tell there was some sort of hanky-panky going on with this activity. It wasn't just to encourage us to make new friends.

On the contrary. We were told that certain colored rubber bands were STIs, and we had to raise our hands to show the exponential spread of them. If you shook hands with this guy, raise your hand. If you shook hands with anyone with their hand raised, raise your hand. And so on. The intention was to show a cute little demonstration of the concept that when you have sex with someone, you're also having sex with everyone they've ever slept with. Six degrees of fornication.

This charming little superstition, that if you screw me then you're banging everyone I've ever screwed, has done more harm than good. In the case of HIV, Russian Roulette was a metaphor I often heard invoked in my adolescence, as though putting a cock in my mouth was as risky as putting a gun in it. *It might go off! Don't swallow semen! Spit it all out or risk getting AIDS!* Except that in an America of random shootings on a daily basis, you are statistically more likely to be shot by a stranger than to contract HIV while on PrEP and/or with a poz-undetectable partner. There goes the Russian Roulette analogy.

Don't panic, though; you're still very unlikely to be shot by a stranger. Gun enthusiasts often claim that the best defense is to have your own gun available and to know how to use it. This is debatable; two guns don't make a sunflower. However, whether you carry a weapon or not, the best defense against being shot certainly isn't to stay home with the covers pulled over your head, and the best defense against HIV is not to avoid sex altogether. Right now, the best defense is to get on PrEP and use it as directed if you think it's right for you. It's not flawless, and it isn't foolproof, but the way to deal with that is this: don't be foolish with it.

With the use of PrEP to prevent transmission, highly effective HIV meds that make viral levels undetectable in the blood, and condoms and conversations to avoid other STIs, the fact here is that the safest sex is not abstinence. The safest sex is a rollicking good bout of hot, beautiful, thoughtfully prepared-for sex. I know that the planning part can be a buzzkill for many, but think of all the other things we do to prepare for sex: shaving, douching, buying meals and presents, begging, etc.

Condoms break. PrEP doesn't. There's no critical moment in the bedroom (or wherever) when you are faced with whether to take your pill or not, how your partner will react, whether the pills are expired, and where did you leave those pills anyway?

Of course, Truvada doesn't prevent other STIs, but as my friend David Schmader wrote on Facebook, "It also doesn't paint your house." Incidentally,

David is HIV-positive. His husband is not. PrEP has opened up new and vital realms of intimacy in their relationship. *That* is the power of PrEP, and I recommend you read David Schmader's writing on the subject.

If you hadn't figured this out already, PrEP is also for the health, peace of mind, and pleasure of HIV-positive people, dissolving much of the stigma and undoing three compounded decades of fear, shame, and rejection.

Sex is normal. Sex is good for you. We were told for decades that HIV is prevalent, easy to catch, and agonizing. Then, people just seemed to get over HIV. Straight people don't usually talk about it if they aren't in health fields. We think it's contained now that it's treatable. The unspoken thought is that regular people, including middle-class, married-with-kids gays and lesbians, don't get HIV anymore.

We're not all flailing around worried about blood transfusions or stepping on dirty needles like we were in the '80s and '90s, which is of course a good thing. Well, Seattle people are still afraid of stepping on needles, but this is a port city. We're a heroin town.

With breakthroughs in HIV treatment, people are less afraid of the disease. For those with access to proper treatment, it becomes a chronic but manageable illness, not a death sentence. That's wonderful, but it's also tricky. There's a much-needed and well-earned sense of security accompanying the existence of HIV, but that doesn't mean you can't or won't get it. Most people in America, young queer people included, have fallen into a comfort zone of ignoring the disease and its risk factors simply because we don't see people dropping dead from it everywhere. When's the last time a beloved celebrity passed away from complications due to AIDS? Willi Ninja is the last celebrity I know of who passed from complications of AIDS, and that was a decade ago. But as my friend Javier, a gay middle-aged white man who read an early draft of this book said, "Who's Willi Ninja?"

But HIV is still out there. People still contract it, and in no small numbers. We just weren't hearing much about it. Then PrEP came along, and we have a new topic reigniting the HIV conversation.

The rise of PrEP has been covered by such disparate news sources as NPR, the Huffington Post, and Fox News. Even Buzzfeed treated it as actual journalism—none of that "Twenty-Two Celebrities Who Are Talking About PrEP And Aren't Porn Stars" stuff.

If you want to balance your corporate journalism and federally-approved science with real life stories, you can check out the Facebook PrEP groups like "PrEP Facts: Rethinking HIV Prevention and Sex," "#TruvadaWhore" (which is much more informative and anti-shame than the name would indicate), or "PrEPaccessNOW." You can also look at blogging sites like myprepexperience. blogspot.com (not recently updated, but recently enough to have insightful personal stories).

If you're an American, I also recommend looking at a mix of European and Canadian news sites, which can offer different perspectives and different priorities for public health standards. Nations outside America often have doctors and scientists who are less worried about being sued, and therefore they have a wider range of possibilities for research and prescription. That can be a double-edged sword, but the information is there.

You can Google the hell out of PrEP, and you should. This book is not the first or last word on it, and I am not a doctor. Do your own research. Use common sense. Don't forget to relax. Sex itself is good for you. It's HIV and other STIs that are harmful to you, and now we can treat them and prevent their transmission in a variety of ways. We have to get past this idea that sex is bad. You don't have to live in that reality anymore.

Welcome to my reality.

WE'LL START WITH Josh. I think my relations with Josh are great examples of some highs and lows of my Truvada experiences, and he and I represent two different ways and reasons people use PrEP.

I met Josh on Scruff. Or was it Grindr? Josh is tall, he's burly, he's cute as a box of puppies, and he's a big ol' bottom. Of course I was infatuated with him.

Hanging out with Josh and negotiating sex revealed much to me about what many guys feel about PrEP. We did the dance of a thousand text messages during the first week of flirting. Both of us were interested, but not, like, *interested* interested. It's easy to get distracted on the apps.

I soon ran into him at a bar called R Place, where we'd both shown up to watch *RuPaul's Drag Race* with friends. Coincidentally, R Place is the bar where Robbie Turner, a season 8 contestant, headlined weekly shows, and we got to hear Robbie lament constantly about how he still hadn't been a contestant, and what a great contestant he would be on that show, and how he would just *excel.*

Josh and I met unexpectedly in person, got a sniff of one another's pheromones, and decided to actually follow up and go on a date. We planned out a lovely summer evening at the beach. We had some food from the PCC deli, some cupcakes, and a nice bottle of rosé, because I am classy as fuck.

We watched the sun set at Golden Gardens park. We kissed while others barbecued and played Frisbee around us. I thought about how good it is to live in the time and place I do, where I can kiss a man on the beach, surrounded by straight people, and it's no issue.

As we drove back to his apartment, he asked me questions about what it's like to be on PrEP. He was waiting to get his prescription. This has become one of the most interesting things about being on PrEP—talking about it can be a great way to build a connection with someone. It's personal enough to create some trust and disclosure, it's a hot current topic that's relevant to most gay guys, and since it leads directly into questions about safer sex practices, talking about it can be a form of verbal foreplay. By the time we got to his place, we were on quite intimate terms.

Josh's studio apartment was quite lovely, all tidy and mature (aside from the bathroom). I had not expected the crosses and other Catholic flourishes here and there, nor the collection of knickknacks shaped like chickens. Everyone has their thing, I suppose.

I didn't expect true love, but I wasn't writing him off entirely. We made the usual small talk, and then he suggested turning on a movie. At this point, I should confess that I've never understood the strategy of turning on a movie when both of us are 90% certain that we're going to have sex. Do we really expect to make it past Act One? Is it a way to avoid the small talk, because we don't know what to say? If background ambiance is needed, turn on the radio. Then again, that can get also get distracting. I recall one sexual encounter during which, every ten minutes or so, commercials would cut in, with inane and boner-murdering jingles like *One Eight-Hundred CARS 4 KIDS, C-A-R-S, CARS 4 KIDS!* That's a tough tune to give head to.

It's not that difficult to have sex without a movie on. Start with cuddling, kissing, maybe some massage. Why do we require the dulcet voice of Miss Dolly Parton in the background? As heaven is my witness, Josh put on *9 to 5* as our background movie for sexy time. I had the privilege of listening to Dabney Coleman sexually harass Jane Fonda while I was trying to get it on with Josh.

Jesus tap-dancing Christ. *9 to Fucking 5?*

I should note that the first time, we did not have full-on intercourse. It was definitely promising, the kind of shy but enjoyable sex two people have when it's their first time together. I find that many people are rather polite and/or shy the first time—"How about this?" "Would you like it if I did it this way?" "Can we turn the lights out so you don't see the areas of my body I'm ashamed of?" et cetera. First time sex with Josh was better than average, as I recall, and I was interested in doing it again.

Then I had to pack up my house the following week and put it in storage. I was going to move to a new apartment, but that couldn't happen yet, and I needed to be out of my current place.

I went into an intense six-week writer's workshop called Clarion West, where I challenged myself to focus entirely on writing and reading new work at the exclusion of sex and dates. I'm glad I did so—I made amazing friends, met influential editors, Skyped with Neil Gaiman, and I wrote a fun set of new fiction stories.

Josh texted me a couple of times during the workshop to ask if I'd come over and top him this time, but I told him truthfully that I was being strictly celibate until the workshop concluded. We chatted a bit through text, and he flattered me by telling me that sex with me was the most intimate he'd ever had it. I'm glad that I could give him that; I got some allusions from him that he hadn't had many previous sex partners, or perhaps he'd had his share and they were fleeting, selfish, distant, or any manner of non-intimate circumstances. For whatever reason, I stood out to him in the way I touched him and held him.

That makes me proud. I aim for sex to be intimate. I think I have an intimacy fetish. Much more often than not, I want the person I'm sharing my body with to feel like a friend. I want to have the kind of sex that makes us both want to see one another again. To hear that Josh was missing out on intimacy in his sex life and that I gave him that? That gave my heart a boner.

I was all about seeing him again when I got out of the workshop. One night during the final week, we sexted, and it got pretty hot. Sexting an author isn't a bad idea, you know. He told me how much he wanted me inside of him, the things we'd do leading up to it. At one point during the sexting, as I tried to make the protection element sexy, I mentioned condoms. It's important to know that by this point, Josh had started taking PrEP.

There are condoms in this fantasy? he texted back.

I live and I learn. *Picture whatever you want,* I texted. We moved past that and finished, but I didn't forget his comment.

I made it successfully through Clarion West without getting distracted by sex, although I did sign onto Grindr one morning at five a.m. after pulling an all-night writing session. I only signed on to find someone to talk to (at least, that's what I told myself), something to keep me awake until the household met for breakfast at eight o'clock, but holy quivering shit. Five a.m. on Grindr is even more soul-shattering than five p.m. The summer sun was dawning, but the darkness was in all of our underpants.

I took myself downstairs and made some black tea with a shot of rum. I'd never drunk at dawn before, but it was clearly a far better option than whatever cold-cooked bathtub meth they were peddling on Grindr.

I lost Josh. He'd been so puppy-dog about asking me multiple times to come see him, but he must've moved on. From there, it was back to text tag for six months, neither of us trying particularly stridently to make a date work. He even sent me an adorable bedroom pic. Josh has absolutely mastered that pose of lying-naked-on-my-stomach, staring-into-the-camera, legs-kicked-up-and-crossed-behind-me, bootylicious-as-you-please. I even sent his own pic back to him weeks later, with the message, *I still want in on that.*

I still want you in this! he replied. Still, we didn't make a meeting happen.

After six months of these shenanigans, I was back on Grindr for another bout of being basic, knowing of course what I was getting into. The will is strong, but the texting thumbs are weak. Or maybe the other way around, whatever.

Hey! Josh messaged me. *We still need to make some great sex happen.*

I'm down for that, I replied. *When are you free?*

Tonight? came the reply. *Or maybe this weekend.*

Bingo. I was going to have another big plateful of Josh. *I'm having dinner with my friend near your place this evening, how about I check in with you in a few hours?*

His reply was enthusiastic: *Great! Talk to you then.* <emoji of smiling purple horny devil face>

A few hours later, as promised, I texted him: *Checking in. Is 10 o' clock too late to come over? I might be done earlier.*

I didn't hear back for several hours, until after 8 p.m., then: *I have to get up early.*

I replied, *I think I'll be done here and available by 9.*

I'm sorry! he wrote, *I already jerked off. I assumed you would be busy.*

Oh well. Another night, another dream. I still wanted to see if we could finally make this happen, so I texted him the following Sunday.

> **EJP:** *Hey Josh. You wanna try again for tonight?*

> **J:** *Sure!*

> **EJP:** *Great. I'll check in with you this afternoon. Also—I'm actively using condoms even though I'm on PrEP. Thought you should know. Let me know if that's a deal breaker.*

> **J:** *I'd prefer not to, but it's fine.*

> **EJP:** *Thanks. I've been going to some health events and it looks like STIs are going up even though HIV is down.*

> **J:** *I respect your commitment to your health* <smiley face emoji>

Now, wasn't that a mutually respectful conversation? I felt great about meeting up with Josh, at long last. Alackaday, when I did text to check in that afternoon, I got this reply: *To be completely honest with you, too much planning around sex turns me off. Same with condoms. I want to be excited but I'm not. Also,*

I'm suuuuuuuper hung over today.

I sighed and replied, *No worries.*

That was the only mature response. Neither of us owes the other sex. Everyone is allowed to change their mind; that's part of consent and respect.

Nonetheless, when I wrote "No worries," I was more accurately thinking, *You little punkass dingleberry, you flake out every time, you text me out of nowhere telling me you really want me to come over and fuck you this time, and then you come up with excuses, and I am so done with you.*

But I didn't text that to him, because my mom and dad raised me right. It's not really my business why he turns down sex, even when he reaches out to me for affection and then decides not to follow through. Josh isn't some beautiful but vapid nincompoop. He's quite smart, and there's a very sensitive fellow behind those crystal-blue eyes. Josh is a complicated person, and he makes his own decisions.

One of those decisions has been to get on PrEP. Josh can now feel better about eschewing the planning of sex in favor of the spontaneity that turns him on so much.

My friend Gwen, one of the beta readers for this book, is a devout feminist and staunch critic of rape culture. She surprised me in her response to the Josh anecdote by saying the following:

"I totally get what Josh is saying. Preparing for sex isn't sexy. Delaying the act by negotiating it isn't sexy. Condoms aren't sexy. Even consent isn't sexy, really. We try to make these things sexy, but they aren't. We want sex to be amazing. We want everyone to read our minds and know what we like without us having to state it or negotiate it. But it's never like that."

This helps me better understand why other people hate to plan sex. Planning, preparing, etc., drains the excitement out of it for some. There's a major kink around surprise sex, even and especially what looks like sex without consent. Many people do want to be grabbed and thrown against the wall or onto the bed. A lot of guys certainly do. We see that house-wrecking, clothes-tearing fantasy played out on TV and film all the time. When's the last time you or your partner actually swept their arm across a table or desk and took you on it? There are important receipts and things on there. Jeez.

Personally, I love planning sex. Thinking about it, sexting about it, and so forth turn me on a lot. But there we are again: different people like different things. Thus negotiation. I think Josh and I are great examples of how differently people's sexual patterns are, and how PrEP plays into that. PrEP gives me the peace of mind to have sex with any person I want; it gives Josh the peace of mind to have sex in any way he wants.

Eventually, and by "eventually" I mean a week later, I decided to drop the grudge against Josh. I texted him and asked if he would give me some fundraising advice. He's an expert, and it was a good reason to clear the air.

I might still hook up with Josh. If I do, and it leads to anal sex, I'll probably use a condom. If he refuses condoms, we won't go beyond oral sex. Simple. No pouting, just consent—from both of us, to every act. Even when consent isn't sexy.

That's how I use PrEP.

Two

How I Lost My Virginity In The Age of HIV

30 tablets

Rx only

To UNDERSTAND THE full weight that's been lifted from my mind by Truvada, it's important to understand what sex was like before PrEP came along. My youthful sexual misadventures are far too many to list, as entertainingly wacky as they've been. I'll save that for the sequel to this book. Nonetheless, I'll pick out the formative ones, particularly the ones in which I tried a new sexual experience.

But before we can discuss virginity, we should get a handle on what sex even is. When I think of all the guys with whom I've had oral sex, most of them never followed by anal sex, I wouldn't say a single one of those encounters *wasn't* sex. If it wasn't sex, why did we have orgasms?

Even so, we can look at sex acts as levels of intimacy. Much like a person can come out in stages (to yourself, to a trusted friend or family member, to close friends and family, to the general public), most of us lose our virginity in stages.

At the time I'm writing this, I'm still not sure I've entirely "lost" mine. I don't really believe in male "virginity." By extension, I don't support the idea of female virginity, because virginity was historically about women being property, whether of their fathers or their husbands. The idea that a woman's virginity is a source of power for *her*, not for a man, is pretty recent in Judeo-Christian culture. It's older in pagan cultures, wherein virgins could hold a high spiritual status as priestesses, etc.

That's no perfect system, either, as we can see in the myth of Medusa: before she was cursed to be hideous (woe is her), she was gorgeous, and because she was gorgeous and unobtainable, she was raped by the sea god Poseidon. As a high priestess of Athena, Medusa was supposed to stay a virgin. Athena cursed Medusa to be ugly and to kill the men who looked at her, all because Medusa "lost" her virginity in Athena's temple. Even if she wasn't raped (some legends say it was consensual), she was punished remarkably for the double dishonor of losing her virginity and getting ravished in the temple of Athena.

Do not fuck with Athena.

Medusa then became a bogeyman figure in ancient Greek culture, a way for children to scare each other and for parents to make their children be good. This is why virginity equals misogyny for me; it's used to control people's bodies and behavior, particularly female people.

Why do I, as a queer guy who has never had sex with a woman, care about female virginity? Three reasons. For one, I cannot ignore the fact that women around the world are still reduced to property, that their vaginas are examined for signs of previous ownership. For another, I believe that all homophobia is just a specific form of misogyny, punishing men for being "like women," women for being "like men," and gender non-binary people for simply being. Only men are allowed to be "like men," even though women are still punished for being "like women." As a gay/queer activist, I can't *not* be a feminist.

The third and most personal reason I care about female virginity is because, at some probably recent point in Western culture, we've developed the idea that men also have virginity. I suspect this began around the same time we started teaching women that having a hymen gives them personal power, rather than giving men power over them. Then how the hell do we track male virginity, especially when a cock is going into a mouth or ass instead of a vulva?

I not only have sex with other dudes, I'm also never completely sure which body part is going to enter what other body area. Therefore, I have no sodding clue what defines the loss of male virginity. Where does that precious essence go? Is it somewhere with all the socks I've lost between the washer and the dryer?

Straight people developed a metaphorical series of sexual stages during the twentieth century, which could be used as their own stages of virginity loss:

First Base: Kissing, with tongue or without.

Second Base: Feeling a woman's breast and sometimes nipple sucking (fun for people of all sexes).

Third Base: Genital contact, from masturbating one another through oral sex. It's unclear if dry humping with clothes on counts as second or third base.

Home Run: Penovaginal intercourse. I dare you to use "penovaginal" in a sentence this week, preferably on Twitter. Tag me @evanjpeterson and #PrEPDiaries.

Of course, baseball metaphors are also applied to queer sexuality: Pitcher and Catcher, Switch Hitters, Playing for the Other Team, Playing for Both Teams. But the "bases" don't really hold up to same-sex or other queer relationships. They don't even hold up in straight relationships anymore—no one's sure where anal sex belongs on the bases. Third base? It's not considered "real sex" by a lot of straight people, particularly young straight people. Then again, it's considered so extreme and kinky by others that it's way beyond a home run—it's breaking the bat in half when you hit the ball.

Fetishes, known quaintly in some circles as "paraphilias" (as in, "next to" or "beside" traditional sexuality), are difficult to assign a base to. Perhaps the prefix "para-" is very well suited here. If you get off on rubber gear or spankings or foot worship, well, I don't know what bases to assign.

All of this to say: it's all arbitrary and pretty stupid at that. I have no idea when or if I lost my virginity by anyone's standards but my own, and my own standards say that I never had a virginity to lose.

The first time I kissed a guy was at the Saint, a nightclub on State Road 84, out near US1 and the Fort Lauderdale Airport. I don't recall his name. The kiss wasn't spectacular. He was the assistant manager of the club, which made him a glorified doorman/bouncer. He was always sweet to me when I'd go in. He and the other staff just let me in with my regular ID for months. This was before the city cracked down on underage admission to the gay bars after some drunk teenager got slammed by a car on Las Olas Boulevard outside of Cathode Ray. That was the story going around, anyway.

I had been going to the Saint since November 1999. I had just come out to my dad. Mom had known for years, but I didn't trust my dad until I was seventeen. They weren't separated, either; we all lived together.

Dad actually advocated for me to go out late on weekends to a dance club when my mother wanted me to just do kid things like all the other kids—drama club, haunt the mall, etc. Dad is a really good guy. He has his faults, but he's always encouraged me to try new things and grow and learn myself, including going out late to gay dance clubs when I was seventeen. I *may* have finagled the facts a bit in order to get their permission, but Dad's no fool. When I'd get ready to go out at night, he always went down his list with me before I went out:

"Do you have money?" "Do you have protection?" "Okay, be safe."

I was remarkably safe. I didn't dare try to drink underage, even though I could've easily played "Hey Mister" and gotten drinks by flirting. I also didn't try to have sex with anyone. I was afraid of HIV and unusually afraid of getting raped. I was a starry-eyed, freckled rube, but I at least knew what I was.

One night at the club, I was getting some air outside, feeling bold and frisky. I'd been to the Saint probably four or five times, and I wanted a dude to kiss me already.

The door guy—let's just assign him the name "Mark"—was doing his job of not very much other than checking ID. Not a lot of riffraff to keep out in those days. I thought Mark was a handsome motherfucker in his all-black, wannabe-high-end bouncer get up. Why do they have bouncers wear ties? For the glamour, darling?

Mark and I made small talk. The Florida winter air was a cool sixty degrees on my sweaty skin, and I turned the conversation towards what kind of guys he liked. I was so bold when I was a kid, before codependency really kicked in and I lost much of my confidence.

I asked Mark, "What do you think of me?" I don't recall his answer, but it was positive enough for me to maneuver into a kiss. Somewhere in the building, ecstasy tablets were bought and sold. Somewhere in the city, someone was wrapping a car around a tree. Someone was putting a bullet in someone— maybe themself. Meanwhile, a few feet from State Road 84, I had my first kiss with a man.

The kiss lasted for about ten or fifteen seconds, not much tongue, but nice on the lips. Sparks didn't fly, and I don't recall my mind being blown the way it was the first time I kissed some of my men. I barely knew him. But I was almost a man, and he was an experienced man, a handsome man, and Annie Lennox was singing "17 Again" while the older gays got misty-eyed and blamed it on the soap bubbles from the foam party (remember those?).

I can't remember what transpired afterward. I don't remember if we exchanged numbers, but I doubt it. This was just before cell phones became ubiquitous. Most of us had landlines. Maybe he got wise and decided I wasn't the chicken worth going to jail for. Whatever happened, I have zero negative memories. Thanks, Mark, for being the first man to kiss me. Thank you, Mark, for not taking advantage of me in the ways you could so easily have done.

I had officially made it to first base with another dude. Two snaps for this little queen.

In February, John Goodwin died from complications of AIDS at the age of 41. Goodwin was also the Fort Lauderdale drag queen Dana Manchester, a beloved performer, philanthropist, and pillar of the community. People would die due to AIDS every day, but John/Dana was a local celebrity. The popular local bar Georgie's Alibi later named their Manchester Room after her. Within three months of coming out and debuting into the Fort Lauderdale LGBTQ community, I was surrounded by people mourning their friend and hero.

The summer between high school and college is a bit of a blur. I came into a little bit of money from a dead relative, and it meant that I didn't have to work for a year to pay for my car or my cover to get into the Saint and the Copa and the Coliseum and all manner of other kitschy gay Fort Lauderdale nightspots that no longer exist. I don't remember how many dudes I kissed between that night at the Saint and my arrival at Florida State University. It could easily be none. I was still terrified of HIV, and I wanted to have a real boyfriend with whom to explore sex, not a string of strangers. I wanted sex to be special, or at the very least something done in mutual care and affection. I was holding out for that.

I do recall looking into the mirror one night, getting ready for a summer's night out. Seventy percent of being a club kid is about getting ready. I was going through a red eyeshadow phase at the time—menacing glamour! Menacing!

My father passed by the bathroom and looked me over. "You know, that belt doesn't go."

Was he teasing me? Teasing each other was our way of working out the tension over me coming out, both of us still figuring out how we felt about it.

"It's the best belt I have."

Dad and I locked eyes in the otherworld of the mirror. "I'll loan you one of mine."

My father is so fucking cool sometimes.

A FEW MONTHS later, in the crotch-stinking heat and humidity of Florida August, Dad and Mom moved me into Bryan Hall, a dorm on the campus of Florida State University in Tallahassee. My plan: Get to fuckin'.

I was eighteen, a freshman at the school *Playboy* magazine had christened the number one party school in the country, and I had never so much as jerked off with another guy. I was starting to get cranky. I was ready to dive into dating someone and start fooling around.

The dorms opened for students to move in a full week before classes began. This gave all of us freshman some time to make friends, find the buildings where we'd take classes, get ripsnortin' drunk, occasionally die from heat stroke and car accidents, and begin a long succession of poor sexual decisions.

I had a few friends from my LGBT youth group (thank you, Fort Lauderdale Pride Center!) at the school with me, and we marched down to the LGBT Student Union and joined up. We were hanging out in the office when two grad students stopped by with their younger friend Justin.

Ooh lar lar, thought Evan J. Peterson.

Justin was tall and nerdy, but he had a certain confidence of posture and movement. I wanted a Justin of my very own.

When he showed up at an apartment party two nights later, I made sure to talk to him. We were young. We were horny. We both spoke rudimentary French. It was enough.

Justin and I hit it off. I mean, we hit it off like an aspiring benevolent slut hits it off with someone with zero dating or sexual experience. Justin and I went out for about two weeks, seeing one another frequently, which seemed really promising when I was eighteen. I don't recall much of what we did socially. I know we went to dinner together at least once, because we both got sick from the spinach-artichoke dip at the restaurant.

The artichoke dip incident must've been our second date. Once both our stomachs had settled, our teenage horniness really kicked in. We made out like we owed each other money. We stayed mostly above the waist, but it was hot. Maybe we jerked off together. Maybe we didn't. I don't recall. One thing I do recall is telling him that I was concerned about HIV. Without saying a word, he leapt off the bed, and like a butt plug out of a hat, he manifested a yellow sheet of paper that read, among other things, "HIV nonreactive... No presence of HIV antibodies detected." The date was very recent.

That made me feel better, but nothing other than a period of abstinence before and after testing could settle my fears completely. I'd had the "safe sex or abstinence" mantra drilled into my brain for years: in school, at home, in the media, even at the LGBT community center. This was not an easy doctrine to give up. Like a kid who grew up in a devout household and later embraced agnosticism, I couldn't quite shake the superstitions that had bombarded me during my entire adolescence. *Negligence kills. Condoms save lives. The people who get HIV are responsible for their own lapses in judgment.* That last sentiment comes from the queer and straight worlds equally, by the way, but so do those who fight that stigma.

On our third date, I took Justin back to my dorm room to make out. Tonight was what straight people had referred to for decades as "The Night."

My roommate, who could've easily won Filthiest Person Alive in a John Waters movie, was out for the night. Justin and I got down to business.

I had never been naked with another guy as an adolescent or adult. Here he was, lying on top of me, face to face, making eyes. He started talking dirty, and having never done this before, I was totally into it.

He jostled gently side-to-side on top of me.

"What's that I feel?" he asked me. Meaning my cock. Which was hard. Because cocks do that sometimes.

"What do you think it is?" I said as coolly as I could. Damn, I was a smooth character.

"It feels like you've grown a little—"

Wait for it—

"tumor on your stomach."

In the distance, car tires screeched to a halt.

Heaven help me, he kept going. "What do you think we should do about that?" I thought, *Do a biopsy?* but instead I said, "Um… What do you want to do about it?"

He raised an eyebrow and said, "I'll show you what we do with those." He crept down the trunk of my body and put my cock in his mouth. I expected glitter to shoot out of my ears, like the first time I had an orgasm with the shower massager at age ten. I expected my body to break apart into a flock of hummingbirds. I expected my nipples to leak pure vanilla extract.

Instead, I hated it. I don't know what he was doing down there, but it was beyond uncomfortable. It hurt. I don't know if it was the pressure or his teeth or what, but I definitely couldn't orgasm. This adolescent tomfoolery went on for a few minutes, and either he got tired of doing it or I figured out how to move things along. We ended up jerking off together, then glowed and fizzed in each other's arms.

"This right here? This is the best part of sex," he said, holding me close and kissing the summer sweat on my forehead. Justin had several years' sexual experience already. He was the only teacher I'd had so far, and he was a sweet and decent man, regardless of his peccadilloes. We were teenagers. We were working it all out.

One thing I was working out was my pervasive fear of HIV. I knew I'd done nothing truly risky. His cock hadn't gone in my butt or my mouth. I checked my fingers for any bleeding around the cuticle, something that happens often. I tried not to get any of Justin's cum on me. I was vigilant. It made bonding with my first sex partner awkward.

In the following days, I reflected on something I'd heard repeatedly on the MTV show *Loveline*, a sex and relationship advice talk show hosted by Dr. Drew and Adam Carolla. Several young men on the show had expressed that they didn't enjoy receiving oral sex. As a horny teen, I studied the show for future reference and to understand myself. It was one of the only shows on TV that featured real, normal gay people talking about their sexuality without the staging of a tabloid talk show or "reality" TV.

Could I be like these guys who didn't like getting blown? Damn it! I was so looking forward to this big, bold, beautiful achievement of manhood.

The following week was the first week of classes, and I saw Justin once or twice. He told me he had decided to become a drag queen. He had his name all picked out: Candy Cox.

Gross. He even had a witty catchphrase picked out: "Lick 'em and stick 'em!"

Yes. Well. We all know how that groundbreaking philosophy worked in practice.

The drag stuff was all right by me—I'd been dressing up as my drag character, Roxy Roadkill, for at least six months, tail end of high school. What was not all right was Justin's insistence on having acrylic nails at all times from now on. He went to work at the discount clothing boutique in the Tallahassee Mall and knuckle-typed the cash register like he was some kind of bougie girl from the block. They were like Fritos on the ends of his fingers.

I had to break up with him. There were tears. I will never forget his eyes welling up, followed by those words said in his Georgia boy accent, "I think I'm going to have an Oprah moment."

Justin, I hope you're out there happy, healthy, and fierce. You do you, girl.

Second base covered. Third base: halfway there.

AT SOME POINT, I got the conviction into my pretty little head that I should use condoms for oral sex, because abrasions in the mouth *could* make me vulnerable to contracting HIV from a man's semen and pre-cum. I guess I had read that somewhere or learned it in a safer sex workshop, which we had many of at the Fort Lauderdale Pride Center.

I've talked to many doctors and HIV educators about this. Can I or can I not contract HIV from giving a guy head? I've heard contradictory answers:

+ "Technically, yes—but it's so unlikely that you shouldn't worry about it."

+ "We assume so, but it's so difficult to track people having only oral sex and not anal or vaginal sex."

+ "If you have a cut or abrasion in your mouth, then of course you can."

+ "No, you can't. There are agents in the saliva that will destroy much of the virus, and then the stomach acid will get the rest. HIV cannot survive for long outside the blood or semen."

+ "Yes, you can. The tonsils pull it right into your body."

What's a boy to do? I did what any hyper-vigilant gay eighteen year old growing up in the age of AIDS would do: I collected flavored condoms. Banana was the worst—like a Runts candy, but even more nauseous. Just suck an overripe banana dipped in chlorinated water, why don't you. The phallic correlation was not enough to save artificial-banana-flavored condoms. Strawberry was pretty good. Vanilla was the best—subtle, sweet, not particularly flavorful but better than a mouthful of latex.

I tried different flavors in advance. I also tried putting different kinds of condoms on myself. It seemed like a good idea to try these things out before getting caught up in the moment, the way we practice safer sex conversations or asking someone out or for a raise or even measuring our dicks. I tried playing with my butt—fingers, toys. That was fun and different, but I could live without it. Actually getting fucked by another guy was still very intimidating. I decided to just stick with oral sex for a while.

I used either flavored or unlubricated condoms for oral sex with 100% consistency until about the age of twenty, when I gave them up in favor of the

feel of real skin in my mouth and the increased closeness and intimacy of it. I
heard a few (not many) other guys tell me they used the same precautions for a
while before letting that go. Safer sex educators continued to say, "This is a form
of safe sex. Do what feels right to you." As I recall, only one guy ever asked me
to put a condom on for oral sex, years after I'd stopped using condoms for oral,
and I happily obliged.

I began using condoms for oral sex with the second guy I ever hooked up
with: Ben. Nerdy Ben. Adorable, nebbishy, skinny little Ben. He looked kind of
like my dad.

It had been a couple of months since Justin, and no magical boyfriends had
crept out of the North Florida pine forests to grant all of my eighteen-year-old
wishes. I was ready to hook up, and it was Halloween. That is what Halloween
is for, damn it.

I thought I was too broke to buy a cute Halloween costume, and I wasn't
feeling the fantasy of going out in drag. I believed no one would want to have
sex with me if I were in drag. Thus, student-poor and wanting to look my best, I
used a bit of creativity and collected the cigarette butts from around the grounds
of my dorm. I sewed them onto a fitted black t-shirt. I went as an ashtray! I
smelled terrible.

Believe it or not, I wasn't sporting the worst costume at the party I attended.
There was a man wearing only some eyeliner and a sparkly sarong. He said he
was a fairy. He didn't even have wings. He also said his name was Tank, which
is unfortunate whether he or his parents chose that name. What kind of Sarah-
Palin-offspring name is "Tank?" Are we in a John Hughes comedy? Tank was
exactly the person you're picturing: very buff and very short. Hyper-muscular
because he's so short. I really, really wanted to fuck him.

I didn't approach Tank too closely because I believed that no one that hot
could possibly be into me. I lost many opportunities to meet good men that way.
Instead, I gravitated to one of the cute and nerdy guys. He told me his name was
Ben. He was visiting for the weekend from not-too-far-away in Georgia. Again
with the slim and nerdy Georgia boys.

We sat and chatted while the stereo played Britney Spears and Madonna on
the recently popular technology of MP3. Traci, a young woman who aspired to

be an extravagant fag hag, sat down with us and began making small talk. Then she dropped the lead balloon.

"So are you two going to fuck each other tonight?"

I was mortified, and I think Ben was too. We looked at each other like, *Maybe? Probably?*

Ben seemed safe enough to take home. He was a little whiny, a little shy, pretty awkward, but also very handsome. This was quickly becoming my type. I took him back to my dorm.

My roommate, Pig Pen the Soil Monster, was off at some weekend retreat with the fraternity he was rushing. They were a pretty decent fraternity—racially integrated, which in the Deep South was a big deal, and they had an openly gay brother whom I would eventually bonk.

When Ben and I got back to my place, he went into the bathroom to freshen up. He left his wallet on my dresser, and I snuck a look at his ID. One can't be too careful. He was, indeed, of legal age. I also now knew his last name in case anything happened that would make me want to find him later.

Ben returned from the suite-style bathroom chamber that Pig Pen and I shared with our neighbors. One thing led to another, as we both knew it would. I later came up with a formula that if you can get someone to sit on your bed with you the first time you meet, you are approximately 99% assured of hooking up with him shortly afterward. At the very least, you'll make out.

Ben was the first guy I ever went down on. That part of my memory is vague—I don't recall the sounds he made and such, but I know I put a condom on him and sucked him. It was easier than I thought it would be, but my jaw got tired quickly. I later developed the strategy of chewing refrigerated gummy bears to build up my jaw endurance. True fucking story—try it.

After I went down on him for a bit, he sucked me till I got off. Huzzah—I really did enjoy it. It was just a fluke the first time with Justin. Then he asked me, "Can I fuck you?"

Decisions, decisions. Could I go through with that? No. Not with someone who wasn't my boyfriend. I wanted bottoming, of all the things, to be in the context of being comfortable and cared about by the person inside me.

"Ummmm. I've never done that before. I'd rather not do that for the first time tonight."

"Hmm. Okay. Can I rim you?"

No one had ever done that to me, either. It seemed gross. *Who would want to do that?*, thought Little Eighteen-Year-Old Evan J. Peterson. I hadn't even showered in like six hours. I supposed I didn't have to kiss him afterward.

"Okay, sure. How do I—where do I—"

"Here, straddle my face."

He lay back, and I sat on his mouth, facing the wall at the head of the bed. I stared into the face of Dr. Frank N. Furter, clipped from a magazine advertisement for the twenty-fifth-anniversary DVD of *The Rocky Horror Picture Show*. I'd wallpapered my side of the dorm room with such things— Marilyn Manson pictures, printouts of Gerald Brom illustrations, an image of an ancient bas-relief of bird-footed Lilith. I stared at my icons while Ben lapped at my dark poppy.

Like my first blowjob, my first rimjob was also unspectacular. It wasn't downright uncomfortable the way the other first time was, but it was clearly doing ten times more for Ben than it was for me. Perhaps it's because I usually get a lot more pleasure from my cock than from my ass, but years would elapse before I was ever rimmed again. Another guy did it for me about eight years later, one of my many Kyles, when I was about twenty-six. Also unspectacular. Kyle was the first guy I tried rimming, but I've always been kind of reluctant about that. Rimjobs are a bit rustic for my taste. A little too "farm to table" for me.

"Are you sure I can't fuck you?" Ben asked again.

Ugh, this thirsty motherfucker. "I'm sure, Ben. Are you close to coming?"

"Kinda close."

"Is there anything else I can do for you?" I reached back and took his cock in my hand while I continued to ride his face.

He put his mouth back to my butt. "Just this. This works."

He went back to wanking himself, and I let go of his cock. I went back to thinking seriously about my life decisions while getting my first plate job. Saint Frank N. Furter gazed down upon us.

Ben repositioned me to straddle his chest so he could suck me instead. That was better. After a minute or so of that, he said, "Hey—let me know if this is okay."

He put his hands on my thighs and suddenly shoved me down onto his erection. It all happened so quickly—I couldn't tell if the head went inside me or if it just hurt from the force of it. And it did hurt. There was no warning, no lubrication, just a sudden stab at me. I reacted quickly and violently. I lurched my pelvis away from his dick. I balled my hand into a fist and brought it down on the crown of his head. "No! That is not okay!"

I didn't know what to do. I suppose he didn't either. He went back to blowing me. I just let it continue. I don't remember what happened between that point and my giving him a ride back to his friend's house.

When a person is sexually assaulted, it is very common and completely normal to go into a sort of autopilot mode. The mind wants to survive, and sometimes that means pretending that nothing bad has happened. I didn't really "get" that I had just been sexually assaulted in the legal or social sense. My mind said, *Well, that was a shitty thing. Let's just get him out of here quickly.* In that way, divorcing the actions from their psychological significance, I got through the event safely. The impact of what had happened did not hit me until the next day.

As we finished our disastrous sex, the sun was rising. I was done and over it with Ben. I hurried him through getting dressed, and I gave him a ride to his friend's house. I had promised that I would. He was visiting from out of town. Also, I didn't want to deal with the consequences of kicking him out, leaving him to wander my dorm like the lost little fuckwit lamb he was, telling my neighbors God knows what about me.

We knocked on the door of the house. It was about six a.m. on a Sunday. Fancy house, Tudor style, the kind we find tucked into the woods of Northern Florida, big and gauche and inhabited by four or five college-aged lodgers. No one answered our knock. My irritation grew by the minute. Why was this shithead my responsibility all of a sudden?

He talked. "Uh, I think my friend's bedroom is in the back corner of the house. Maybe we should knock on the window?" We walked around the back of the house. We knocked on the glass. Was there movement inside? No one came to the window.

"Evan, would you be my boyfriend?"

God help me. *God help me.* This was still happening. "I don't know, Ben. Can we talk about this later?"

A sexual assault counselor later told me that it's very common for the rapist to ask the victim to be in a romantic relationship. It's common for the rapist to buy gifts and be extra nice afterward. It's the apology phase, the "honeymoon" stage after an abusive episode. It reminds me of a scene from *Girls Will Be Girls*:

Dr. Perfect: "God has given us a second chance, and I say we take it!"

Coco: "You still shouldn't have raped me."

Dr. Perfect: "Really super sorry!"

Ben and I returned to the front of the house. He began ringing the doorbell over and over again. Persistent, that one. A man who knows what he wants and isn't afraid to go get it. Little rapist piece of shit.

After a minute or two of nonstop doorbell ringing, a young woman came to the door and yelled at us.

Ben asked, "Is Jennifer home? She told me to come back here."

The woman at the door said, "No! Jennifer is not home as a matter of fact."

I turned and jogged to my car. "Goodbye, Ben! Get home safe!"

I drove back to my dorm and put myself to bed. I'd been up all night with Ben. I needed my sleep. When I parked my car, I found twenty dollars on the ground. God never closes a door without opening a window.

I don't remember what I did after I woke up. In fact, I don't think it was until the following day that it all really hit me. We were already having consensual sex play. Why wasn't that enough for him? Why rough me up?

My first sexual assault was nothing like I had seen on TV or in a movie. He wasn't some walking mugshot who jumped out from behind a tree. He wasn't some smooth talker who roofied me at a party or a bar. He was a gangly, soft-spoken dweeb with bad posture and little self-esteem, and his face resembled my father's.

I took a rape shower. I had seen such things in films and TV, of course. If you've never had the misfortune of taking a rape shower, that part can be a lot like it is on screen, unlike the rape itself. I cried. I sat there curled up wondering how the hell I let this happen. Wondering if I should tell someone. Wondering if I should tell the police or just work it out with my friends and a therapist.

I had to face a battle of definitions in my head. *Was I raped? It didn't feel like it at the time. I punched him in the head and he stopped. That's not a real rape is it? I got away easily. So many people go through so much worse. He wasn't a family member. I wasn't a child. Do I have any right to say I was raped?*

The sexual assault counselor with whom I eventually worked told me that it's not about whether my head was smashed against the wall. It's not even about whether his dick actually went in. In my case, it's about the fact that I told him not to do something, and then he did it anyway.

I told her, "I feel ashamed. I feel like this is my fault. I feel like I have no right to complain."

"Evan, that sounds to me like a usual reaction of someone who was sexually assaulted."

Hearing that did make things better. I didn't need to just dust myself off and move on. I could certainly stop blaming myself though.

Lest we forget what this whole book is about—I thought a lot during my rape shower about HIV. I knew that Ben had been leaking pre-cum, which I'd heard contains more or at least as much HIV virus as does the actual ejaculation. I knew it hurt when he tried to stuff it in me. Could my skin have torn? What if his fluids got inside my body?

I got down on my knees in the shower and prayed to a God I wasn't sure existed. I kept my eyes shut tightly but the shower spray dripped into my mouth. "I promise if I test HIV-negative, I will never have sex with a stranger again."

At the time, I was desperate, and I meant what I said. This promise lasted about six months. I was very torn between my superstitions and my desires. In the end, I broke my promise, but I also got a new higher power, or maybe just adjusted the one I had to fit my heartfelt values.

I think it was about a week afterward that the tip of my penis started to hurt. Checking myself and my underwear, there was just the smallest trace of what looked like infection. I decided it was time to go and get what we in gay culture call "Tested for Everything."

I was still pretty broke, and I heard that the Health Department would test everything for free, unlike the health center on campus. They would often charge fees, frequently for unnecessary procedures.

I took myself down to the Health Department to let them poke and prod. The building itself looked dismal, like many buildings in North Florida. Not the stately brick buildings I was used to on the FSU campus. No nostalgic Spanish architecture. This was a squat little concrete compound with dim windows that, with the November sunshine, I couldn't see into.

I had never sat in a waiting room for an HIV test before. It was ghastly. I tried to read whatever magazines they left out, but I couldn't concentrate. I wondered about the others in that waiting room. Young people. Poor people. Embarrassed people who wanted anonymous health care.

A poster on the opposite wall read, "We hope you have a POSITIVE experience today!" I wanted to murder the person who came up with that wording.

"Evan?" the nurse called. I got up and followed her into a poorly lit grid of rooms. A phlebotomist drew my blood—just an arm stick. We didn't have finger sticks or oral swabs quite yet for HIV testing, but those were on the way shortly.

After the blood draw, it was time for the rest of the testing. The nurse asked me to strip off my shorts and underwear and stand before her. She fiddled about at the counter, then turned back to me with what looked like a sharpened cotton swab.

"What's that for?" I asked like a perfect horror film victim.

"I'm going to insert this into your penis to get a culture swab."

I shrieked, "What!?" with an audible interrobang. Then I groaned and consented. "Ow! Owwww!" I whimpered like a child. I felt like a child. She sounded the tip of my penis with the swab and twisted it. It was rough, and it stung me.

If you've never gotten "Tested for Everything," it can include a throat swab (gag), anal swab (dry and twisting), an arm stick (metal zinging as it slides beneath the skin), and a finger stick (the needle snapping into flesh). After I've gotten this battery of tests, I often feel assaulted, my body scraped and penetrated. Luckily, in all the STI tests I've had since, I've never had to endure the cock swab again. It's always a urinalysis and/or arm stick—for penis stuff anyway. I still endure swabbing of the throat and occasionally the anus, but at least I'm the one who performs these acts on myself.

Another of my beta readers, Javier, has this to say: "Swab tests? What were those about? As soon as I got a gay doc, it was all pee in a cup, swab my ass, but Public Health only ever jammed a dry swab up my urethra. I swear it was on purpose to teach us sluts the wages of sin."

As the nurse twisted the dry cotton inside my penis, I thought about what an awful experience women must have during a rape kit. I thought about what that would mean for a man.

At least the arm stick wasn't so bad. I'd gotten used to having my blood drawn frequently while on Accutane, a drug that I'd taken to finally clear up my persistent facial and body acne. This was an important experience in my PrEP journey, though I didn't know it at the time. Accutane was a physically dangerous drug, not usually life threatening, though it seemed to exacerbate suicide and depression among its users.

The irony. Accutane was intended to make us look smoother, cuter, more photogenic, to increase our confidence through greater self- (and other-) esteem, and oh by the way, it may also make you want to kill yourself. My Accutane doctor, the "specialist" who saw all the kids on campus who were on the drug, had put me on suicide check-in the moment I voiced that I was feeling depressed about my transition to college (about two months before my encounter with Ben). I knew I was nowhere near suicidal, and I thought the weekly depression check-in calls absurd, but in retrospect I think it was an excellent and mostly noninvasive program to reduce suicide. Then again, this doctor was the same one who a year later calmly handed me a free one-month supply of Wellbutrin like it was a coupon for vitamins. I told her I was feeling depressed that my first boyfriend had left me for someone else, and as Heaven is my witness she said, "So you're depressed because you're gay?"

"No, Dr. S., I'm fine with being gay. I'm depressed because my boyfriend dumped me and then started dating his 'internet buddy' a few days later."

"Well, it's common for gay people to be depressed."

"Yeah, I know, but I'm not depressed because—"

"Here, I'll get you a one-month supply of Wellbutrin. Take this and come back in a month and tell me how you feel."

I didn't take a goddamned one of those pills. I tried to sell them, but who the fuck takes Wellbutrin to get high? They ended up in the trash can with toenail clippings and some jizzed-in tissues.

I'm not sure if the Accutane caused gastrointestinal damage, but I began having horrible stomach pains and irritable bowel syndrome a few months after completing my regimen. This went on for a year: stomach pains that were occasionally immobilizing, daily diarrhea, weight loss. I had to tell professors on the first day of class, "I'd like you to know that I have IBS, and I may occasionally have to leave class abruptly to use the restroom."

Did the Accutane cause this? Maybe. Maybe not. What I can say for sure is that the same Dr. S. told me, "I think maybe you have IBS because your pants are too tight. Don't wear such tight pants."

This person is paid by a major university to diagnose and give medical advice to eighteen-year-olds. Just as she misattributed my depression to my sexuality, she misattributed my crippling stomach pains to my choice in pants, which I suppose was also indirectly related to my homosexuality.

Dr. S. put me on all manner of antispasmodics and other drugs that year. Some helped, and some didn't. Whether they helped or not, I could only get a diagnosis of *irritable bowel syndrome*, which as it turns out is considered *idiopathic*—a non-diagnosis for a spontaneous condition, the cause of which is not understood, and for which all other known or likely possibilities have been ruled out.

Suffice to say, a lot of people looked at my shit under a microscope that year. I didn't have Crohn's or colitis or stomach ulcers or parasites or bacteria or AIDS, as my mother constantly feared.

My mother kept her eyes open for possibilities. She once showed me an article clipped from the newspaper about the spread of hepatitis A among gay men, the symptoms of which had some overlap with my condition. In the article, it mentioned that hep A is usually spread through unsanitary food preparation, but that it can also be spread through mouth-to-anus contact.

I walked into my parents' room. "Do you really think I have hepatitis?"

Mom sat on the bed folding laundry with Oprah on the television. "Well I'm just concerned. I'm trying to help."

"The article says gay guys are getting it from eating ass. I don't eat ass, Mom." At least, I hadn't done so yet. In my prudish youth, I was embarrassed that she'd suspect me of such a thing.

"Well, I don't know what you do!" she moaned, throwing a sock ball into the laundry basket.

In her defense, she was trying to be open and gay-positive when she clipped the article for me. When I went to our family practitioner, he asked me, "Do you shoot up?"

"No! Of course not!"

"Is your urine dark?"

"No."

"Okay, then you can tell your mom you don't have hepatitis. We don't need to test for that. Your stomach trouble is something else."

Eventually, it was Mom who found the solution: acidophilus.

My body must not have had enough of the right gut flora. Whether that was the result of taking Accutane, the stress and anxiety of my first year of college (including being assaulted sexually), both, or neither, it turned out that the only thing that worked—in fact, the only thing I actually needed to do—to clear up my debilitating stomach issues was to take acidophilus and probiotics.

That's it.

It took several months to even out, and I was still prone to cramping spells in high-stress times, but soon after I began drinking acidophilus milk and taking acidophilus pills, my "irritable bowel syndrome" went away.

Now, why have I spent the last few pages telling you about my intestines? Between the Wellbutrin incident, the Accutane issue, and the IBS debacle, I developed a mistrust of pharmaceuticals and Western medicine in general. I had moderate anxiety/depression and crippling stomach pain, and doctors wanted me to pop unreliable pills for these symptoms instead of working on the root causes. Then again, it's Western medicine that's able to test us for HIV and a variety of other STIs. I use Western medicine when it's my best option, which it frequently is.

I've undergone acupuncture for a variety of issues, and it helped me absolutely with some, not at all with others. Herbal and natural remedies have helped me considerably with a variety of internal issues. However, some things require laboratory chemistry. I believe PrEP is the best thing I can do for my body to prevent HIV. To finally make the decision to get on Truvada, I had to get over my distrust of pharmaceuticals and the guessing games doctors had previously played with my body. That was a big distrust to get over. Of the queer guys I meet who tell me they will never use PrEP, about a third of them explain this dissent as a mistrust of "Big Pharma"—the corporate/capitalist overmedication of every physical and psychological issue.

I have deep sympathy with these men and this sentiment. However, I came to the conclusion that if I wanted to finally have peace of mind about HIV, to build romantic relationships with poz guys, to freak freely as well with strangers from time to time, Truvada as PrEP was the simplest, most effective solution.

I have an acquaintance, "Timothy," who is a lawyer as well as an alternative-medical practitioner. The first time I met him, he had been HIV-positive for less than a year. He asked me why I would take PrEP, why I would use a pharmaceutical for a condition I didn't have. He's not the only person to ask me that. Some think this is a profound question, but it sounds more like a trick or a logic trap to me.

I told him honestly that if there were a natural treatment to prevent or cure HIV, I would take that instead. I'm convinced there's no such thing.

Timothy went into a diatribe about how the human body's function is to heal itself and suppress disease, how all diseases are manageable when the body is healthy. The problem with that way of thinking, of course, is that HIV suppresses the immune system itself.

Timothy went on to say that he was treating his HIV naturally. He made a bet with his doctor that he could reduce his own viral load through a combination of meditation and abstaining from consuming things that taxed his immune system: alcohol, allergens like soy and dairy, etc.

In researching this book, I decided to follow up with Timothy and interview him. He said that he had decided to go on HIV medication. I asked him what changed his mind. He told me that screening every single thing he consumed to prevent ingesting something toxic was too stressful, undoing whatever good he did by meditating or avoiding the allergens in the first place.

I really wanted Timothy's naturopathic efforts to work. I wanted to see HIV viral loads reduced to low levels through diet and meditation alone. That's not what I learned, so I keep taking Truvada. I still haven't had any side effects, and if I had, I'd need to reconsider my use. "PrEP tummy" is common, but I never had digestive issues when I started my regimen, and I have, ahem, a rather delicate little rosebud of a digestive tract. Barring pancreatitis, which can happen to a rare few unfortunate folks, the stomach issues clear up after a month, and I've met very few guys who stopped using it just because of the early digestion issues. Even if I were to contract HIV, Truvada is far more effective than eating only bananas and sleeping on a mattress full of amethyst.

It turned out after my penis-scraping trip to the Tallahassee Health Department that the only thing they found "wrong" with me was a simple urinary tract infection. This had apparently come from bacteria in Ben's mouth. *Venus hold my hand.* I took the penicillin they gave me and waited the two weeks for the HIV test results to come back.

I thought about my prayer. *I'll never sleep with another stranger again. Just let my HIV test come back negative.*

Perhaps it's a good thing that I don't recall going back to the Health Department and receiving the news that my test was "non-reactive." I do recall running around campus brandishing the yellow printout with its terrible faded gray dot-matrix characters, seeking out friends with whom to share the good news. A dear friend since freshman year, a devout Christian who has only ever had sex with her husband, recently told me, "You were so relieved. I remember your face before and after. I had no idea what that experience must be like. I was so concerned for you."

What I do remember is the next test, several months later. I needed a three-month window to be more accurate, and I marched myself back to FSU's Thagard Student Health Center and had my blood drawn by Miss Shelly, my favorite phlebotomist, the one who'd been puncturing me monthly for my Accutane check ups. I pinched the skin on my knee with my fingernails in an attempt to lessen the anxiety of the needle going in.

"Ain't I stuck you before?" Miss Shelly asked me. "I ain't going to hurt you. I see you pinching that knee."

"Yes, Miss Shelly. I'm just nervous today." I grimaced. Miss Shelly smiled and took my blood as gently as ever.

Another nasty two weeks of worry, then I came back and sat in an examination room to await the results from Dr. S. She was gone a long time. I mean a *long* time. My panic swelled. All I could do was stare at the images on the walls—charts of the human digestive system, reminders to wash hands, etc.

I was eighteen. Damn it all if I got HIV at eighteen from a rape. I thought I'd be dead by thirty.

Dr. S swooshed in the door and said casually, "You're fine." She fiddled about with some paperwork.

This person is paid by a major university to tell eighteen-year-olds if they have HIV or not.

I had to check and make sure I had heard her correctly. "I'm fine, you said?"

"Yes, your test came back negative."

I was so relieved that I wanted to vomit. I wanted the results sheet so I could gloat over it. Also, I wanted to save it in a shoebox under my bed, to have it on hand to show future partners as Justin had done with me. "Don't I get a little yellow sheet of paper?"

Dr. S looked at me with suspicion. "If you want to have it."

I did want to have it. That was none of her fucking business. This is the same person who told me my pants were giving me diarrhea because they were too tight.

I got the sheet and went back to my dorm. I thanked God and remembered my prayer and my promise. I didn't hook up again for several months, and then it was with a friend—who gave me pink eye, but I didn't have HIV. Didn't have it.

I'd gone through my first excruciating HIV test and period of waiting for results. The rite of passage was completed.

I've looked for Ben on Facebook a few times in the past fifteen years. I looked for him the day I started writing this part of the book. When I got the search results, I could have clicked each profile that matched his name, trying to see if I recognize him. Instead I thought, *Why do that?*

Why does one look for his rapist on Facebook? I guess I did it to prove that he really exists. That it really did happen.

I'm no longer easily triggered. It happened so quickly, the actual physical part. Penetration, or the attempt at forcing that, is the briefest part of a rape. The greater trauma is the emotional process that follows.

This was my second sexual experience ever. The first time I ever went down on a guy. The first time I let someone rim me. The first time a man forced me into sexual contact I'd already said "No" to.

After getting assaulted by Ben, I lost all interest in bottoming. Even when that interest came back, it has been a huge deal to me, something requiring immense comfort and trust with someone. But that's simply what is. I've developed a fun and satisfying sex life anyway.

I guess I completed my third base. I felt like I retained as much of my own power as I could. That's something.

I also want to puke when I write about this.

Three

Still Losing My
Virginity Over Here

30 tablets

℞ only

THE YEAR 2000 became the year 2001. New beginnings! What could possibly go wrong?

Before some planes flew through some buildings and changed the world as I knew it forever, I had some more awkward sex. I had just turned nineteen.

There was Jackson, who was very cute, but our personalities clashed. We tried going on a date, but that didn't lead to anything. A month or so later, I had an itch to scratch, and I asked him to come over to my new single-occupant dorm room and bang around.

I'd finally petitioned my way out of living with Pig Pen. I wrote a strongly worded letter to the housing department stating that our room was a health hazard, and they found an open single-occupant room with private bath, which had been set aside for disabled students. I was saved from having to face a human wallowing in his own filth four feet from my bed every day. How that young man got laid with real live actual women, I shall never know. He got that room all to himself and probably died of gangrene in it. I got the new room with the private bathing chamber, which Jackson helped me christen.

I put a condom on Jackson before going down on him. I was genuinely, deeply concerned about contracting HIV from oral sex, even before I developed my canker sore issue. Jackson didn't want me to wear protection for oral, which was fine by me. I had a great time with him, but we never hooked up again.

Then there was Rusty. Rusty seemed like a good idea at the time.

When I reflect back on what it was that led me to fall hopelessly and recklessly in "love" with a grown man who still went by Rusty, I'm at a loss. Wrong boy, right time? He was cute, and he liked me. As a nineteen-year-old "virgin" gay guy still reconciling HIV, a sexual assault, sexual frustration, and the need for love, that was enough.

Rusty and I met right at the end of my freshman year. He was beautiful, mixed Irish and Cherokee. He looked a lot like Hayden Christensen. He had a gorgeous cock and a serious alcohol problem. I was smitten.

I seduced him at his best friend's birthday party. A mixed group of gays and straights played "adult Jenga," which was like regular Jenga, except every piece removed from the tower had a sexy dare on it. As I recall, I took the dares and not only licked his nipple but also put my hand down his pants, right there in front of God and everyone. You're only nineteen once.

Some frat boys—the Q Dogs from Omega Psi Phi, one of the more macho frats—wandered into the party, saw Rusty and me making out, and said, "Whoops! Wrong party!" and left with a shred of grace. Rusty and I eventually went to the only private place in the house, the laundry room, where we proceeded to make out and fondle each other in the dark. When we emerged, my normally styled-to-death hair was mussed to filth, a pretty good indication among my friends as to what I'd been up to behind closed doors.

I had been dating Jerry, the birthday boy and Rusty's best friend, for a couple of months, but all we ever did was kiss. Jerry would pick me up, take me out to dinner, pay for everything, tell me how great I was, make out with me, then drop me off at my dorm. I finally confronted him and asked if he wanted to take things to the next level, or any level for that matter. He finally exercised some boundaries and made it clear that I was too young for him, and it wasn't going anywhere. So I seduced his best friend, Rusty, because fuck you, Jerry, this is my booty chronicle, and also because I wanted to prove to myself that I could.

We reap what we sow. Rusty and I spent a whirlwind week sleeping over, sexing together, and otherwise canoodling in between my cramming for final exams. He looked amazing in the shower. He refused to let me shampoo my own hair. I thought he was what Mama Peterson would call "a real mensch."

I even told my Intro to Philosophy teacher that I was falling in love for the first time, and that this was very inconvenient during finals week. Professor Cohen said that love was always worthwhile, even during finals week. I should've just dated her instead.

Rusty made no complaints about me using condoms on him for oral sex. Like Jackson and Trainwreck Ben, he didn't want me to wear one while I was in his mouth. He seemed perfectly at ease keeping the sex oral. My plan was to lose my virginity with him, at least as a top.

Rusty and I had such explosive chemistry that by the end of the week I started desperately trying to figure out how we could date long-distance while I was back in Cooper City, Florida for the summer. I couldn't convince him to wait for me. Why should he? We'd only "dated" (read: blew each other tenderly) for a week. This was four months of separation, and since we were both young and doe-eyed monogamists, that meant a lot of frustration and heartache until we could reunite.

I was required to move seven hundred miles and live in my parents' house for the summer because my mother didn't want me to waste money living off-campus if I wasn't taking classes. It didn't help that my parents were going through a bad patch in their marriage and chewing one another's guts out half the time. I felt I was forced to break up a good thing with Rusty just so that I could live under their roof and listen to them bitch at each other for four months. My IBS got worse. I got a job working as a credit card telemarketer, and that kept me out of the house during the weekdays. It also paid my cover charge at the nightclubs where I whiled away the summer nights.

That was the summer I developed mono and subsequent chronic canker sores. The sores seem to be connected to mononucleosis and that cluster of diseases, but they don't seem to be contagious. I say "seem" because the clinical knowledge of this condition is woefully behind. As if I wasn't concerned enough about the possibility of contracting HIV from oral sex, now I could easily develop an ulcer in my mouth at any point. And then another. And then two more. For a fucking decade and a half this went on. Then I got on Truvada.

I am forever grateful that Truvada has suppressed these almost completely. I eat, I drink, and I suck cock like a champ, all without consistent suffering or fear of HIV. Thank you, Gilead Sciences, for this blessing. You really should market this Truvada stuff to chronic canker sore sufferers. I do still get flare ups, but they're abnormal. When they happen, I cool it and take care of my health.

My mother cared for me during my abysmal bout of mononucleosis. Maybe I got it from Rusty. Maybe I got it from one of the guys I made out with that summer at the Coliseum or Cathode Ray or the Saint. Or maybe I got it from a toilet seat. It doesn't matter. What matters is that Rusty immediately started dating someone else in Tallahassee, because the poor little daffodil couldn't be alone for more than a week. The struggle is real.

I was so new at this, and I wanted so badly to have a boyfriend at last, that when Rusty's new boyfriend dumped him, I convinced him to spend the final month of summer waiting for me to get back.

The next few weeks passed quickly. He sent me a mix CD of songs that meant a lot to him, including Lisa Loeb's cover of "Leaving on a Jet Plane," Ani DiFranco's cover of "Amazing Grace," and Tori Amos's "Hey Jupiter." It was the kind of music that fell in the Venn diagram overlap of music beloved by both gay men and lesbians. I got very into Tori Amos after that, and "Crucify" was my go-to breakup song for years. I'm tempted to crack a joke about that, but it speaks for itself.

The final song in Rusty's mix was Etta James's "At Last." He wrote that this song made him think of me, how he felt about me, how he couldn't wait to rest his forehead against mine again and greet me, how he couldn't wait to be my man.

I can't believe I fell for that cockshit.

When I got back to Tallahassee and moved into my newest dorm room, Rusty and I immediately spent three days together. My poor, unsuspecting new roommate Joe thought I would be scarce that year as I repeatedly slept at Rusty's place. Joe would later have sex with a real, live woman right in front of me while he thought I was asleep, but at least he was tidy and well-groomed to a fault. He always smelled excellent, and he once let me borrow his polo shirt for a job interview. He was a good guy overall. I put him through a fair bit of shit that year, come to think of it. I was working through some temporary mental illness brought on by extreme stress, a combination of the breakup with Rusty, the death of my childhood dog Bucky, my parents' continuing relationship tension, and some planes that just happened to fly through some buildings and kill thousands of people. All these stressors combined against me, and I would wake up in the middle of the night yelling at people who weren't there. Poor Joe. Thanks for not freaking out on me, bro.

I think Rusty may have broken up with me because I asked if we could get tested for HIV together before we started fooling around again. He had, after all, been with at least one other person over the summer. I was so concerned about disease that I wouldn't go down on my own boyfriend, even with a condom on him. He sweetly agreed to whatever I wanted, then broke up with me within the week. Then he started seeing someone else the very next day.

Cue Etta James singing "At Last" over a montage of me ugly-crying and cutting up every picture and gift I'd ever received from him. I was so depressed I couldn't orgasm for a whole month—and since I was a mess, no one wanted to help me out with that. I started having wet dreams (at nineteen!) as my unconscious body tried to do what I wouldn't and couldn't while awake.

Then it was September 11th. When would it happen again? Could we ever go back to taking our safety for granted? Should I just throw caution to the wind and fuck every single guy who'd have me?

I didn't. In fact, I didn't hook up again for ten months, other than a failed attempt that got very ugly.

I remember at one point telling a friend in my Folklore class that I hadn't had sex in four months, and she said, "That's, like, three months too long." Then I started dating Thomas.

Again with the long distance. Thomas and I met through a mutual friend the previous summer, right after moving away from Rusty and right before I came down with mono. Thomas worked at Disney World in Orlando, and he got us all in for free on Gay Day.

For those unfamiliar, Gay Day is the occasion at Disney World when thousands of homosexuals and other queers show up to be together in the

Magic Kingdom and spend inordinate amounts of disposable income on things like princess parasols and mini-motorized foam fans attached to spray bottles. Gay Day isn't officially endorsed by the park, but they always know it's coming. There's a surge of rainbow knickknacks and gewgaws and violet tchotchkes as we inevitably exit through the gift shop. Woe unto the fundamentalist families who take their quiverfull of stalwart offspring to Disney on that day.

Once I was back living in Tallahassee, Thomas and I kept in touch. I decided to stop in Orlando for a friendly visit on a regular trip from Tallahassee to Cooper City. Thomas's place was about five hours from Tallahassee, three from my parents' house. I only had to go a little out of my way to get there, and by this point I was crushing on Thomas pretty hard. If he knew it, he didn't mention it, but he was a rather adorably oblivious dope about such things. He played Goofy at the Magic Kingdom, for crying out loud. They're quite into typecasting at the park.

We spent the day at another theme park, then retired to his place. We flirted all day. He held my hand. We decided that the best place for me to sleep in his apartment was in his bed, where I wouldn't be menaced by his three wacky and similarly typecast Disney-employee roommates: Daisy Duck, Haunted Mansion attendant, and Center of Attention.

We watched a movie. I snuggled up to him. We kissed. He said, "Before we go any further, I want to make sure we don't ruin our friendship."

I said, "I don't think it'll be ruined. We're both grown ups. And besides, we aren't really *that* close."

We had a dynamite time. Over the next four months, we grew closer. I went to visit him a couple times a month, and we bonded solidly. I got to try new things in the bedroom, because I was now actually dating someone over an extended period of time, and there was trust. I got to tie him up and blindfold him, my first experience with bondage. When I untied him, we had the hottest sex I'd ever had at that point. Then again, at twenty, my few sexual experiences were on a scale of Decent to Horrifying.

Thomas made sex good again. Sex with him was generous. It was fun. It was emotional, and it was hot. Looking back, it was one of the things that got me through the fallout from the sexual assault by Ben: having sex with someone who actually cared about me, who let me have whatever boundaries I needed. Thomas made me feel safe. We rebuilt my confidence together.

When Thomas told me he was my boyfriend, I felt vindicated. My first real boyfriend, who actually showed me he cared about me. Rusty hadn't been an actual boyfriend. That was a fantasy I'd created. Rusty just went along with it. As we say in the South, "She don't know no better. Bless her heart."

I finally let go of condoms for oral sex in this relationship. He was only the fifth guy I ever hooked up with, but I'd also been sexually active for almost two years. That's quite a bit of latex to ruminate upon. Even when we stopped using condoms for oral, I was still so neurotic about HIV and other STIs that I wouldn't put his cock inside my mouth. I just sort of worked on it all around the outside like corn on the cob. He just let me do whatever. It's a funny image, but I feel sad writing about it. I had so much anxiety about disease, and we hadn't had the "window" period completed between his previous partner and a new test. Even so, it was the best sex I'd ever had, which shows how lousy my sex life had been up to that point.

Thomas and I spent hours talking, cuddling, napping, sucking and licking each other—it was beautiful. He was my first actual love. We were two Pisces manchildren who just wanted to hold each other and sing badly along to "If I Could Turn Back Time" in the car. I should've lost my virginity to Cher, not Avril Lavigne.

Lucifer tap-dancing Morningstar, anything would've been better than Avril Lavigne.

On a swamp-ass August day, I made one final trip down to Orlando to spend some time with Thomas. Did I mention that my forest-green '95 Ford Taurus had a broken air conditioner? On the way, another driver was weaving on the highway. He drove hard into my lane while he was right next to me. I swerved to avoid being sideswiped, but I lost control of the vehicle. I remember the steering wheel of my ramshackle car turning this way and that with its own intentions. The car spun around in a full circle plus another 180 degrees, middle of the interstate, and came to a stop pointed at oncoming traffic. I stomped the gas and drove with purpose into the grass on the side of Interstate 10.

I am so incredibly lucky to have walked away from this. Maybe the spirits are looking out for me after all. It wasn't even an "accident" so much as a fuckup—no cars got hit, as far as I knew. I lost nothing but some tire pressure and peace of mind.

People stopped to ask if I was okay. That meant a lot to me. Say what you will about Florida, but people pulled over to make sure I was okay. After I assured the other drivers that I was fine, they drove off. A minute later another guy stopped just because I was out of my car and catching my breath on the side of the road. He said he saw my rainbow bumper sticker and wanted to see if I needed help. I guess he was gay too, or at least sympathetic. Most people are good people.

Fat lot of fun this day was turning out to be. The knowledge that I was going to see Thomas, that I'd soon be in his arms and everything would be fine, bolstered me. I needed his kisses. I needed his love.

I stopped to have my tires checked out in Gainesville. Minimal repairs were needed. When I got to Orlando, Thomas was behaving strangely. I had a bad feeling. Maybe it was because his roommate's folks were visiting. We didn't linger in the living room.

We went to his bedroom and closed the door. It was our custom to have sex immediately. I mean immediately. I could barely get my shoes and glasses off before he undressed me sometimes—he'd toss me gently over his broad, tall shoulder and carry me like a nelly caveman into the bedroom. I'd ask, "Do I smell okay? I've been in the car for hours." He'd say, "You smell great" and proceed to suck my heart out.

Today, he was very quiet. I asked him what was going on. Then he broke up with me.

"Really? Like, really, Thomas? I almost died today. I drove here for five hours—six if you count waiting at Tire Kingdom—I almost died, all so you could break up with me? We couldn't do this bullshit over the phone?"

He got all embarrassed. "Shhh! They'll hear you in the living room!"

"Oh, whatever. I cannot believe this shit. Maybe this is good that it's over. You're always broke. You never buy me anything. And you never come visit me. I'm always making the drive down here."

He apologized profusely. I accepted that the long distance wasn't working out. He told me he cared about me and had wanted to make it work, but he needed to be with someone who lived closer. Someone he could see more often. This was a legitimate complaint, one I couldn't fix. I wasn't about to drive down there every single weekend like a chump. I had a few standards, even back then. Like two or three at least. I remembered that I had agreed, at least implicitly, not to ruin our friendship.

I was coming to visit for the weekend, not as an overnight stop on my way to see my folks. It was too late in the evening to drive all the way back to Tallahassee, and Thomas wouldn't turn me out. He said I could still sleep there. We went out to dinner—some nondescript assembly line Chinese food that was one step up from the mall, like P. F. Chang's or something gnarly like that.

Over dinner I said, "You know, I'm kind of relieved. I want to be with you, and I care a lot about you, and I have a great time with you. But you're right about the distance."

Looking back, what I really felt was that I couldn't do better than long distance. My number one crush had become my boyfriend. He was a better friend than boyfriend throughout the relationship—emotionally supportive, especially about the sexual assault, but not very available to spend time together. He repeatedly broke plans to pick up shifts at the theme park. He was paying off some kind of debt. I put up with all of this because I wanted nothing more than to be in a romantic relationship with someone I cared about who also cared about me. Plus he was super hot.

After the check came (split of course), we both went to the men's room. As we urinated side by side, I said, "Since I'm already here, can we just pretend we're still boyfriends until I leave tomorrow?"

He leaned over and licked the back of my neck. "Sure."

We got back to his place. He was still worried that his roommate's family would be wandering around the apartment like ghosts at the Haunted Mansion. There was probably some sort of stipulation that the family didn't know the roommate was gay (he certainly seemed self-loathing in his opinions on his own sexuality), and they shouldn't know that the guy lived with gays. Even so, boners called for polishing.

Thomas and I retired to his room. He put on the first Avril Lavigne CD,

Let Go, which he'd picked up while we were at the mall. This provided a sound buffer for our conversations and the breakup sex that seemed like a sure thing.

Avril Lavigne on repeat. God help us. You're only a manchild once—unless you're a manchild for the rest of your life, which I suppose is technically a very long "once." But that was one thing I loved about Thomas: his childlike enthusiasm for stupid yet harmless things.

The album rolled through "Sk8er Boy," "I'm With You," and "Complicated." We talked. We made out. We got naked. Ironically, it was the best sex we'd ever had, surpassing even the bondage experiment.

Thomas never complained that we never went past oral sex. He liked topping and bottoming equally, but he said that oral sex was a wonderful thing and he wished he could personally thank the Neanderthal that first came up with the idea. On previous visits, we had discussed the possibility of him being the first person I would top, maybe even the first person I'd bottom for. He was my first real boyfriend, after all. It felt right. He never pushed the issue. He said he always had a great time with me, whatever we did.

On that night we broke up, we'd been fooling around, and he looked at me and said, "I do have one regret. I wanted to be your first."

I looked into his eyes with a mixture of amusement, irritation, and excitement. "You're such a dork. All right, Captain Obvious. Let's do this."

Thomas was the first guy I ever topped. I was pleased that he loved it. It's not difficult to top well; think about your bottom's pleasure more than your own for a moment and see what they enjoy. It's all just a bunch of rubbing, anyway. Read the body.

I, on the other hand, didn't get much out of it physically. It was awkward for me, even though I liked making my man feel good. I've always liked guys taller than me, and Thomas was a big boy. Six-foot-two, two hundred ten pounds, and all sweetness. I, on the other hand, was five-seven and a buck forty-five. We had sex face-to-face, but it still looked like a Welsh Corgi fucking a St. Bernard.

All this was set to the caterwauling of Miss Avril Lavigne, who interrogated me over and over as to why I simply had to go and make everything so motherfucking complicated.

I wondered if it was Lavigne or the condom that prevented me from having a better time. Or, you know, feelings and stuff. I'd never used a condom for actual anal sex before, and I didn't know pleasure-enhancing tricks like putting a little lube on my cock before putting the condom on. I've since found better fitting, better feeling condoms, but as I'd later discover, it's not so much the condom itself that determines how much I enjoy topping someone. There's a mix of things—connection, passion, mixing in some other turn-ons during the actual in-and-out. That first time with Thomas was a bit like my first blowjob from Justin, as my cock disappeared into someone's body and I wondered why I didn't like it more, if I'd ever like it more, if I was actually a bottom and just too goddamn afraid to explore that.

The point I want to get across, after all that torrid confession, is that I used a condom for my very first full-on fuck. I don't want to just call it "sex," because sex is so many things. Thomas and I had been having sex for months, but that sex wasn't intercourse. This time, I was inside him, where I'd wanted to be for a long time, and I put a condom on despite the fact that we were both recently tested for HIV and asymptomatic for other STIs.

Historically, this was back when we were still encouraged to get tested at a three month point and then again at a six month point after our last "risky" sexual contact. Most young sexually active adults do not wait six months between sexual encounters. Thomas had been with someone else within the six month span, before he and I started dating. I was concerned, even with my sweet and goofy Thomas. Concerned enough to put a condom on myself for my very first "home run."

I loved Thomas. I loved myself—I think? I wore a condom to protect us both. Would I put on a condom now to have sex with someone I've been dating for three or four months, monogamously, with a non-reactive STI panel recently completed? I doubt it. It depends. PrEP is a huge boost to my peace of mind. There are other diseases to consider, but they're generally curable or manageable. Sometimes I think people just enjoy being afraid of things, regardless of science or logic or glaring inconsistencies and contradictions.

Thomas and I are still friends to this day, though we talk very infrequently. He's married now. They just adopted two kids, and when I saw that on Facebook I shit the bed. Nothing like your first love adopting two kids to make you really sit the fuck down and think about your life choices. Then again, Thomas was always a romantic. This was always his plan.

   And that's how I finally "lost" my "virginity," whatever that means: awkward breakup sex with my first boyfriend after nearly dying in a car accident, to the tune of Avril Lavigne asking and asking and asking why I was making things so convoluted—complicated—whatever, Avril Lavigne is terrible.

Four

Love and Butt Stuff

30 tablets

R̥ only

AFTER THOMAS, I pinballed around from one lousy hookup to another. I even made self-deprecating jokes about it all: "Oh, I don't have boyfriends; I have flings that last too long," or the self-fulfilling prophecy, "I'm kind of a one-date wonder."

There were some bizarre and torrid experiences—the time I had sex with one of the original *Hellraiser* Cenobites at a horror convention, for instance, or the Man With No Urethra, or the drunken three-way that was more like a two-way with a spectator. #BeenThere.

I didn't have another boyfriend for eight years. There weren't any HIV scares in those eight years, nor would I date anyone HIV-positive. I somehow made it through three years of graduate school without having sexual intercourse with anyone, despite my sporadic hookups with a Gothamesque rogues' gallery of misfits, tramps, and thieves.

I wanted butt sex to stay special, something I did with someone I'd actually gotten to know. I never got to know anyone well enough during those years. I'm not demisexual (i.e., only sexually attracted to those with whom I've built an emotional bond). In fact, I can dream up extravagant sexual fantasies about people I see on billboards. They could be dead for all I know.

I wanted topping—and eventually bottoming—to be *good* the next time, good in a way it hadn't been during breakup sex with Thomas. Eight years crawled by, and I had far more serious relationship issues than where to put my penis.

Somehow, in November 2010, I ended up with Lane. This surprised both of us. I'd met him about six months earlier through a Craigslist ad.

I don't want to spend much time on an aside about Craigslist, but those who've read this far may realize how difficult that restraint is for me. Suffice it to say that I did a teeny-tiny little bit of tricking around on Craigslist, and absolutely nothing that happens through Craigslist surprises me. Cannibal murder/suicide pact? Well, they did meet on Craigslist after all. It's times like these I'm actually grateful for Grindr.

But hey, I met Lane! And Lane is wonderful. I had put an ad up looking for a date to accompany me to a zombie-themed prom. I stipulated that I was gay, that gender was unimportant, and that it could be purely platonic, but if we liked each other we could make out.

What the hell did I think I was doing?

"Dear Craigslist: I'm a lonely gay horror fan and none of my friends will go with me to zombie prom. Who will be my date? We don't even have to be romantically compatible. Just come with me. I don't have enough friends. Also maybe we'll have sex."

Thank goodness no one murdered me.

Lane responded with something like the following: "Hello. I would like to go to zombie prom. I have a partner and we are monogamous, so it will be platonic. I really want to go to zombie prom, and he won't go with me."

We met for coffee and then went to see *Metropolis* at the outdoor theater in Seattle's Fremont neighborhood. I had to make sure he wasn't a cannibal, after all.

I thought Lane was a strange little creature. Not my type. Nope. No sir. He had no job, he had been homeless for a period of time, he had some strange traits (like wearing no colors other than blue), and he was a genius. He was fascinating. I kept hanging out with him.

One day, after I'd decided he was safe, we were ditty-bopping around the university district looking for people to watch. We'd just bought tickets to go see Gorillaz on tour for *Plastic Beach*, which is still one of my favorite albums. I'm not sure exactly what happened, but there was a moment when I looked at Lane and realized, *Whoa. Lane is totally hot. When did that happen?*

A few weeks later we went to the concert. Lane was in a bad mood. He and his partner were breaking up. Lane felt like he was being held back from the life he wanted due to his partner's specific needs. The werewolf in me smelled blood.

He felt much better after the show, and we went to my house to hang out. I made my move.

"So, are you about to break up with him, or did you two already break up?"

"Ugh. I told him we need to break up, but I guess we haven't officially yet."

"But it's over?"

"Yeah. It's over."

"You wanna make out?"

Smooth. Mother. Fucker.

He spent the night. He spent the night several times a week for months. Things escalated quickly from kissing and cuddling to sex. We fell into a great groove together. It was some of the best sex I've ever had. After a few weeks, I told him about how I hadn't topped anyone in years, and he said, "I think you need to fuck me. I think you need to fuck me *right now*."

Praise Venus. He could not get enough of me. I would've bottomed for him, but that's not really his thing. In fact, that conversation went something like this:

"Hey Lane? Maybe you should top me one of these days."

"Nope. No no. We have a deal. I am the one who gets fucked around here." He took off his pants and underwear and climbed onto my bed. "I am getting fucked tonight, Evan, and you are going to fuck me. Take your clothes off, stud."

Oh, Lane. Such a bossy little bottom.

We used condoms every time, which was more for his protection than mine. He'd only ever had one sex partner. I, on the other hand, was up to about forty by then. I was twenty-eight years old.

With Lane, I finally got to enjoy topping. No, "enjoy" is an understatement. We did all the things we could think up that we'd never gotten to try in the past with others. We both loved it when I came inside of him, face-to-face, forehead-to-forehead. I loved the faces he made. The hubbub about this kind of sex, the kind where one person is inside another, was all true—straight, gay, or otherwise. The average human brain must be wired for this.

"Do you feel love for me?" I asked him after a couple of months. We were lying side by side in our underwear, but we hadn't started fooling around yet.

"Yes. Even though you told me not to."

I rolled over, smiling as much out of amusement as embarrassment. "Did I really tell you that?" I ran my fingers through his curly, dyed-auburn hair.

"Yes. You told me not to fall in love with you. The first time we had sex."

"Fuck. I'm sorry. I do remember that now."

Why was I such a goddamn little fuckup at letting people love me? Here was someone who actually wanted to love me after years of loneliness, and I'd told him not to. Maybe that's why Lane was my first lover ever to tell me he loved me. Not even Thomas had said that out loud.

"Lane, when I told you not to fall in love with me, I was telling myself not to fall in love with you."

He looked at me with his stank face that he puts on when he's entertained by something absurd. "Why would you do that?"

"Because you had just ended an eight-year relationship. Because I was trying to protect myself."

"Well, I love you. It didn't work."

"I love you too, Lane. Thank you for loving me."

I got teary.

"Hey, don't cry, stud. I still need you to fuck me stupid tonight."

Lane and I took a relationship break when he went to India for four months. That was excessive. He loves Indian men, and even though I wanted him all to myself, I encouraged him to go sow some oats overseas. He deserved to find out more about what he liked and wanted. I also wanted to be free to sex around Seattle while he was gone for so long. And how many people do you think I hooked up with while he was gone? *Not a one.* The gods of sex and love are funny like that.

Lane came back in late spring. Priorities had changed. I told him I didn't want to get back together. I was afraid he'd hate me. But he loves me. He agreed that we shouldn't get back together, and that this was no big deal. We had some raucous breakup sex and moved on.

He lives in New York City now, and he's had the same monogamous boyfriend for several years. Lane is one of my internet people—people who actually understand what the internet is and how it works at a mechanical level. He keeps my website domain registered. For that alone, I love him.

SHORTLY AFTER LANE, I met Brandon, with whom I became hopelessly infatuated over the single month we dated. It wasn't pretty, and I'm not proud. It was very much like the Rusty incident, and it created a tidy bookend around a messy period of my life.

I was living in a different reality than Brandon. Maybe I needed to go that far into codependent madness before I could break the patterns I was in, but the relationship with Lane had been so loving and normal (for once) that I thought I was immune to fucking it up that soon with someone new.

On our final night together (I had no idea it would be our final night), Brandon and I agreed that we trusted and cared about each other, and he told me he wanted me to be inside him. So that happened. There was so much lead-up, all that emotional and psychological fanfare going into the act, the Big Anal Fun Show and Heart Loving Extravaganza. I wore a condom, of course. I asked him to be my boyfriend during the afterglow. He said something noncommittal like, "Yeah, sure."

He woke up from a nightmare in the middle of the night and said he had to go home. Then he broke up with me three days later. He told me that he couldn't be in a relationship with anyone at that point, and he was so depressed, and his world was falling apart. Then a month later he was dating one of the backup dancers from the touring cast of *Aladdin the Musical*, and the two of them soon moved to New York and got engaged.

I went a little crazy. Like beyond Rebecca Bunch on *Crazy Ex-Girlfriend* kind of crazy, because Rebecca is crazy enough to think she's happy most of the time. This was approximately a 60/40 balance of sane to crazy, where I was constantly thinking about him and how angry I was and how hurt, and maybe

I would have long angry conversations with the mental figment of him when no one else was around. That's how I ended up in twelve-step recovery.

After breaking apart emotionally, I had the opportunity to put myself back together in a new way. That's when I started dating HIV-positive guys.

Five

Interlude
(In A World...)

30 tablets

R only

LET'S SPEND SOME time in an alternate reality. If you've never done this (and if you're queer, how have you never done this?), it's pretty easy. Turn off the part of your brain that wants everything to add up and stay realistic. We might call this your Inner Cynic. Send your Inner Cynic to Whole Foods to spend a lot of money on free-range, fair-trade, gluten-free shampoo or something.

With that little voice out of the way, let's step through our *Star Trek : X-Men : Doctor Who* warp portal and go to Earth Beta, where HIV never became an epidemic. Let's say they found the Truvada formula very early, leading to both the undetectable status and PrEP. Everyone had access to it, and people took it seriously. HIV never got a foothold anywhere in the world.

You wake up one morning next to your true love. Your phone alarm is ringing, playing "Don't Funk It Up," the new single from Sylvester featuring RuPaul and Grace Jones. Jones recently divorced Arthur Ashe.

Sylvester is in her seventies—she transitioned a few years ago but kept her stage name—and she's still a high-energy performer. She's currently on tour with Arthur Russell, Patrick Cowley, and Fela Kuti. You think happily of that night you and your sweetie saw her in the Cockettes Reunited tour a few years back.

You hit snooze on your alarm, roll over, and kiss your sweetie.

Over breakfast and coffee, you read some entertainment news. Dorian Corey and Willi Ninja are suing the LOGO network for copyright infringement. Octavia St. Laurent has refused to get involved.

Alvin Ailey is collaborating with Peter Allen on a new ballet based on the long, successful life of designer Willi Smith, whose designs were recently worn by Eazy-E at the Met Gala. Eazy-E and the other NWA members have been in talks to turn *Straight Outta Compton* into a Broadway show—a collaboration with *Hamilton*'s Lin-Manuel Miranda. Eazy-E eventually settled down and married Kimora Lee Perkins, and they're still together.

It's your day off. You decide to make a grocery run. In the car, you listen to an audiobook of Isaac Asimov's latest posthumous novel, a prequel to his *Foundation* series. Asimov has only been dead for five years, but the treasure trove of his unpublished work keeps on giving.

On the road, you pass a billboard for Halston's new men's fragrance, Z-2017, modeled by Tom Hardy, the spokesperson for the men's clothing line as well. Halston lost his edge at some point during the '80s (see also: JCPenney), but he went on to reinvent himself and become the richest clothing designer in the world. Like a rock star reinterpreting his own songs, his newest line is all about the nostalgia of his own early hits.

Speaking of which, another billboard is splashed with the face of Freddie Mercury, still handsome after all these years. Queen is coming to town. You make a mental note to get tickets the moment they go on sale. Mercury's been covering Bowie songs at every show since the latter's death from cancer, and rumor has it he and Klaus Nomi are recording a tribute album to Bowie. Jobriath, having come back from obscurity in the '90s, may guest on it as well.

At the grocery store, you overhear two university students talking shop in the bread area.

"Can you believe Michel Foucault is still writing? He must be, like, a hundred."

"Oh my God, that's super ironic that you say that, because his latest book is all about the history of aging. Did you know he's married to Tony Perkins?"

"Tony Perkins from *Psycho*? No shit! I thought Perkins was married to Rudolf Nureyev."

"Swear to God, Ashley. He actually left Nureyev to be with Foucault. He's like, really into Europeans apparently."

"Ugh, way to go, exoticizing white people."

"I know. Microaggressions."

Kids these days.

You finish your shopping and see that the cashier's lines are mercifully short. You get into line and look over the magazines. Derek Jarman's newest film, a biopic of Leigh Bowery starring the artist as himself, is up for Best Picture. There is criticism that Bowery isn't old enough to have a biopic, and that his life has been so public as to make a biopic redundant.

"That's just it," Bowery recently told Katie Couric. "People think they know me because of the nature of what I do. But I don't even know myself most of the time."

You pay for your groceries and drive home. You decide to turn off the Asimov book and just listen to the radio. An ad discusses a nearby art museum doing a Keith Haring retrospective, from his "radiant baby" days of simplified human figures through his later work as a digital artist and costume designer. He designed the set of Katy Perry's most recent tour. He's making a comeback.

You come home to the love of your life, and you are grateful to be alive.

"Honey! Let's get tickets to Queen!"

This is a world in which some of our most promising artists and heroes never died in their prime. This is a world in which the gay and trans rights movements weren't set back decades by the sudden onset of a plague. This is a world in which gay marriage has been legal in America since the year 2000. Maybe there's an openly gay or lesbian President or Prime Minister somewhere. Maybe there's a trans First Lady.

No one has heard of Ryan White or Pedro Zamora. They are happy and healthy and unremarkable.

This is a gilded scenario. Many of these amazing people would be dead by now of other causes. Many would've stopped doing anything interesting by now, or else be hoeing the same row they have been for decades. That's not the point.

This is a fantasy of what could have been.

Imagine if we hadn't spent all this time and energy and money and heartache on a plague of miseries, and instead spent it on art, science, innovation, and community.

Six

Super Power:
Undetectable

30 tablets

R only

PART OF MY recovery process was to begin an Internal Family Systems mentorship with my friend Everett. IFS is a mental health modality that involves a lot of talk therapy, but it's talk therapy that's far more in-depth, active, and effective than the old Freudian couch talk. It changed my life dramatically for the better.

My favorite thing about IFS is that it takes away stigma around mental processes and habits. It takes things that are usually considered pathological and makes them simply actions and habits. Instead of calling myself obsessive, codependent, etc., I simply have habits and patterns of behavior and thought. These habits and patterns were developed early in my life to deal with trauma, stress, etc. They're self-defense mechanisms that have stopped doing their job of keeping me safe, and they've instead been interfering with my peace, happiness, and success. From there, it's not so difficult to resolve them, bit by bit.

Everett and I grew very close during the intensive coaching and mentorship. I turned to him because I could tell that going to twelve-step meetings and going to a counselor were not enough to get the job done—they helped considerably, but I was still obsessing, still lonely every day and very angry about it. I didn't just want to talk about my feelings. Those familiar with my journalism know I'm extraordinarily good at talking about my feelings to anyone whose ear I can bend. No, I wanted to go deeper into my mind and find where and when I learned to think and act like this, and unravel that if possible. So that's what we did.

Everett was a Buddhist monk as a young man, and like many gays in the clergy, he ultimately decided he wanted to have a life beyond self-denial in the pursuit of spiritual gratification. So he came out. Now he teaches people how to have a normal, pleasurable life and still achieve inner peace without becoming a monk. He's also an avid BDSM enthusiast who runs his own sex and bondage gear store online. Plus he's the sweetest, gentlest person you'd ever want to meet. He's broadened my perspective on many things.

Everett helped me heal the persistent loneliness, disappointment, and frustration that fueled my obsessive and compulsive codependent patterns. Once that was achieved, we discussed new ways for me to approach dating. It helps that Everett is an older gay man, someone who lived through the AIDS crisis, whose first partner died of complications from AIDS. One day in mid-2013, he asked me, "What are your thoughts on dating HIV-positive guys?"

I sat in his little office, the soft glow of the lamp reminding me of every therapist's office I'd ever been in. Unlike most of those spaces, Everett's office has an altar with sage, crystals, tarot cards, and all sorts of other arcane things that make life worth living.

He offered his pleasant, passive stare and waited for me to answer his question. I gripped the plushy armrests of the chair. "Oh, I don't know. It worries me. I'm scared to."

"Are you aware of what 'undetectable' is and what it means?"

"Um…it means that the levels of HIV in a guy's blood are really low, but he's still technically contagious, right?"

Everett scratched his white beard and turned to his computer desk. "I want you to read up about it. I'll send you some links. Undetectable status is really common now, and the rates of transmission are extremely low. Extremely. There are partner studies in which none of the participants got HIV from their undetectable partners, even without condoms."

"So are you saying you want me to start dating poz guys?"

He turned back to face me. "That's exactly what I'm saying. If you're serious about having a real long-term relationship, you need to stop ignoring that huge chunk of the queer population."

I squirmed.

Everett went on. "I think you could get a lot out of dating a poz guy. For one thing, they tend to be serious about their health and their path in life. They stop fucking around with so many petty distractions. They're more responsible. And, since I know sex is important to you, poz guys are often better in bed."

"Shut up. Really?" I looked down at my hands. I had a ragged cuticle on my thumb, usual for me, and there was a little dab of blood. An open wound.

"In my experience," Everett said.

I looked back at him. He smiled that benevolent, peaceful guru smile, the one that usually accompanies a statement about getting royally laid. I said, "Well…I don't want to stop using condoms."

Everett waved his hand in dismissal. "I'm not suggesting that at all. That's your choice. But get informed. I foresee you having a great time dating the guys you've been overlooking."

I stepped out from the warm glow of Everett's office into the gray Seattle day. Deep in the suburbs of the Wallingford neighborhood, I took a walk. I passed the little makeshift book-exchange boxes that look like birdhouses filled with books. I plucked out a water-damaged volume called *Sacred Sex*. I would later return this unread. There are only so many hours in a day, a week, a month, a lifetime.

I pulled my iPhone out and signed into Scruff. There were the usual suspects, but I was technically in a different neighborhood than my home in Green Lake, so the local feed picked up some unfamiliar faces. I decided to do a search for profile names that contained a plus sign.

For those who need the demystification, the [+] sign on a profile means "HIV-positive." Many guys on the apps have used the plus sign, especially in brackets, to immediately denote their HIV status. This is a strategy for filtering out those potential suitors who won't date/hook-up with someone poz. It's an effective strategy indeed, the other side of the "no femmes/blacks/Asians" trend on the apps. You can sort potential matches quickly, weeding out the insincere. I know drag performers who use drag photos on their dating and hook-up profiles for the same reason.

I'm quite pleased to see that in the last few years, as PrEP has become more and more common, the [+] has been decreasing in its prevalence on my apps. I believe this is a clear correlation. One's HIV status is becoming less and less of a stigma, which is a very good thing for HIV-positive people. Scruff in particular has added a stats option to tell readers that you're on PrEP, or you use "treatment as prevention," which is an explicit euphemism for being poz-undetectable. By the way, treatment as prevention is often abbreviated as "TasP," which should not be confused with "Truvada as PrEP." I certainly confused the two initially.

As the [+] has waned, it has been replaced by a new symbol: [=], which denotes that the man behind the profile has equal interest in meeting HIV-positive and HIV-negative guys, and he treats them equally. Off the apps, the equal sign is used to denote equal rights, particularly marriage equality (see the divisive Human Rights Campaign), but on the dating and hook-up apps, it's usually a reference to being unconcerned about HIV status.

Such symbols are nothing new. They're part of the ever-evolving code of gay shorthand. Like any subculture, especially subcultures with a history of hiding in plain sight, gay guys have an elaborate and pliable slang and shorthand to assist in covertly sharing information quickly and explicitly. This has gone on for over a century, well before Oscar Wilde and his wee gang of sighing cocksuckers all but invented the public stereotypes of the Male Homosexual.

My new curiosity about dating HIV-positive men led me to do a symbol term search on Scruff, and I took an immediate liking to a guy whose screen-name was "Nick [+]." I looked over his profile: in addition to being tall and broad and adorable in the face, my favorite combination of physical traits, he was clearly very smart and had a charismatic sense of humor. He also stated clearly that he was "undetectable."

I said to myself, *Evan J. Peterson, I dare you to message him.*

When that went well, it soon became me telling myself, *I dare you to ask him out.*

Here's the thing about breakthroughs in HIV medication and the subsequent effect on HIV status: whereas for decades there were three HIV statuses (HIV-positive, HIV-negative, and "I don't know my status"), there are now at least two more—"poz-undetectable" and "negative on PrEP." Nick is poz-undetectable, and after my talk with Everett, I finally got it through my skull that this meant he was highly unlikely to "give me" HIV. It also meant he was quite unlikely to die young from the complications of a repressed immune system.

We met up for our first date at a lake two blocks from my home. I spotted him from a hundred feet away as he looked around him, obviously looking for me.

We took a walk. It was a beautiful day, not too hot yet, but green and rich in sunshine. Straight couples walked their offspring in front of us. Androgynous teenagers with terrible Seattle hair rode past on bicycles and skateboards. It was perfect.

We made a side trip to the PCC market to pick up some picnic food. I probably had some kind of high-fiber but low-fart salady thing. Something with farro in it. After eating, we lay down in the grass and watched the clouds. It was a gorgeous day. I dared myself to kiss him. That went very well.

So we went back to my house, and we had fantastic sex for about two hours, and it was amazing, and the sun was setting by the time we were done, and there we were in each other's arms, and we were kissing, and we were turning, and he was above me and then I was above him and this went on and on and I let myself be there with Nick, and I noticed that his eyes were two different colors, one green and one brown, and I only held back a little because I was still afraid of HIV.

When we were done, I sent him off into the sunset like a chunky, baby-faced cowboy.

"I'm dating someone HIV-positive," I told Everett a couple of weeks later at our next session.

He perked up. "Wooooooow. That was quick. How's that going?"

"Holy shit, Everett. I really like him. He's handsome, he's tall, he's sweet but not, like, a doormat. He says he loves how I smell. The sex is great."

Everett gazed at me, proud of his handiwork. "Congratulations! What does he do?"

"Interior design, of all things. But I think it's pretty industrial, for chain stores. He has to lay out floor designs with outlets and light fixtures and all that glamourless shit. He's not picking out swatches of damask or anything."

Everett chuckled. "That would be interior decorating."

"Right. Well, that's what he does. Also, he rimmed me and violet lasers shot out of my taint. No one has ever done that in a way I liked before. I mean I almost cried a little, it was so good. I think something inside me shifted. A spiritually transformational rimjob. Can you believe that?"

Everett cocked an eyebrow. "Can *I* believe it?"

I always just assume that Everett has done pretty much everything. He's the kind of person who could turn an amethyst crystal into a butt plug for telepathic sex, and it would work.

Nick and I continued dating. He was very patient with me as I worked on my HIV fears. It wasn't his job to assuage them; it was mine to get over. It would be rather irresponsible for me to expect him to do the intellectual work on that. Nick and I kept having sex, and I was still wary about where Nick's load ended up when he came. Rationally, I understood that "undetectable" meant an extremely low transmission risk, but I still had that '80s/'90s generational fear of HIV. To be completely and scientifically frank, "undetectable" is gauged through blood testing, which might not accurately reflect viral loads in semen or vaginal or anal fluid. That was a big enough gap in the data—small and inconclusive, but big enough for me to build a superstition inside it, regardless of what the partner studies have shown.

It was 2013. I wouldn't discover PrEP for another year.

But I was so into Nick. He said many of the right things: that I was the kind of person he'd stay friends with, even if dating didn't work out. That was realistic. There were some misgivings on both sides: I didn't like the fact that he was freshly out of a recent relationship, while he as an atheist didn't like the fact that I pray. To me, our beliefs were completely compatible. He suspected otherwise.

The chemistry between us kept up. I tried new things with him, new kinks like electro play. I helped him move a washer and dryer into his new apartment. He pledged $100 to the Kickstarter campaign for my second poetry book, *The Midnight Channel*. It was the highest pledge anyone gave. He even talked up the Kickstarter campaign on his highly explicit and kinky Tumblr blog. Nick and I really had something going there.

The day I helped him finish moving into his new place, effectively closing the chapter of his previous relationship, we had another lengthy, intense round of sex. I zapped him good with that electro wand. He did some new things with me that he'd been hesitant to do. So did I.

Then he ghosted. Maybe the actual move to the new apartment shook him up, made things more real for him. Who knows.

I was angry and offended; he had stated explicitly that we would stay friends. There is always the slim possibility that someone is in a coma or dead or kidnapped by Cossacks when they abruptly stop communicating. But people held in a gulag don't update Facebook.

The usual inner critic popped in to question my every romantic decision:
How do you keep finding these people?
Why didn't you see this coming?
Why didn't you hold back more and make him work to be with you?

I moved on. I don't usually hold grudges against people unless they seriously fuck me over—stalking, rape, theft, the illegal things. Ever made your stalker cry in public? I have. To suddenly cease communicating altogether is manipulative and worrisome, but it's no capital offense if two people have only been dating a short time. It warrants a frustrated eye roll, not a broken heart and an angry rant tagging him on Facebook.

A few months later, Halloween showed up like the mainstream Pagan holiday we need it to be. I didn't understand how much we need it until I moved from Florida to a place that has actual seasons. As things get dark and damp and gloomy in Seattle, we need a festival that celebrates and affirms life while also stepping into the darkness. Just as Yule or Christmas or New Year's Eve mark the return of light into darkest winter, Halloween/Samhain marks the journey into darkness as a necessary part of the cycle of life. People still honor the traditions of the masquerade, dressing up as the very things that frighten them.

We've also found the sex and fertility in death and fright. While Halloween is an opportunity to dress up as monsters and phantoms, it's also an opportunity to be something we can't or won't or "shouldn't" be during the rest of the year. Men of all sexual orientations go out in drag. Women voluntarily and enthusiastically objectify themselves on their own terms, for the thrill of it. Just look at the oft-ridiculous market of "sexy" Halloween costumes. Sexy witch. Sexy alien. Sexy mouse. Sexy french fries. Sexy police officer. Sexy #BlackLivesMatter protestor. Sexy Card Against Humanity. Sexy TurDuckHen. Sexy Ebola Nurse.

I swear that last one's real. Google it.

That year, 2013, I split the difference between ghoulish and sexy and went out as a Cenobite. For those unfamiliar, the Cenobites are the pain-worshipping torture monks from Clive Barker's *Hellraiser* series. The Pinhead horror character is their leader, but there are many of them. Cenobites all bear some form of extreme body modification, from a carved grid on their skulls to a mouth stretched unnaturally into a baboon's sneer. Doesn't sound terribly sexy, does it? What's so damn sexy about the Cenobites is their coolness, not a James Dean cool but a Hannibal Lector cool. They're all androgynous in black leather and vinyl priests' frocks. They conduct a form of extreme sadomasochism that is fundamentally voluntary; one has to call on them before they pay a visit. As Clive Barker himself has said, Pinhead doesn't do one decent thing in ten films, yet women still want to have his babies. There's something strikingly arousing about the combination of danger, androgyny, and coolness. Think Dr. Frank N. Furter meets Ted Bundy. Most folks are not into this. However, the folks who get off on this fantasy get off hard.

I dressed myself as a Cenobite. I whited out my face and chest and shoulders. I slicked back my undercut and whited that out, too. I had just helped my friend Anne move, and I'd inherited her black vinyl prom dress. I adapted this with a black vinyl corset over it to create my Cenobite frock. Anne also lent me a tarnished but beautiful key. My Cenobite concept centered on the idea of keys as a torture device. I put the key on a chain around my neck and drew a few bleeding keyholes around my face and chest. I drew some autopsy stitches on my bared torso. I have an excellent fake blood from Ben Nye ("fresh scab") which looks like utterly authentic congealed blood when it dries. I used this to touch up the wounds. I gathered some along my bottom lip. Voilà! Belle of the ball.

I lined my eyes in a little red to make them pop. I took some selfies, stuffed my ID and cash into my corset, and gave myself the final pep talk in the mirror.

"Either no one is going to want to fuck you, or you're going to meet someone who's completely infatuated by this. Either way, you're beautiful."

It's not about who likes us. It's about if we like ourselves.

Then it was off to the Cock Pit—not to be confused with any other queer venue called the Cock Pit in any other city in the world. The Cock Pit is a private venue, a warehouse-style queer artist commune tucked inconspicuously into the Capital Hill gayborhood of Seattle. You would miss it if you didn't know where to look for it. They throw some of the best Halloween and New Year's Eve parties I've ever attended. I got to the Cock Pit early because the line can be killer and there's a maximum capacity. People live there, after all. Once in, I kissed the usual cheeks with the art queens and costume designers and dance phenoms and djs and homeless kids and drag queens and punks.

I immediately ran into Ian Awesome. Ian is an activist, a journalist, and an anarchist. They're a prominent figure in the political anarchist movement. I forget what Ian was wearing—likely something pink on pink on pink. They do love their pink. They had their best friend Kent in tow. Kent wore a smart suit, but he wasn't clearly any particular character. Don Draper perhaps?

Ian introduced us, then went into a story about when they were in the military and they got to piss in Saddam Hussein's toilet in the dictator's palace. The toilet was apparently made of gold.

Ian skipped away to get a drink or flirt with someone or object to something, and Kent and I got to talking.

"I love this look!" he told me.

"Thank you!" I sipped from my mystery punch. "Do you recognize what I am?"

He took half a step back and eyeballed me. "Not sure. Are you a vampire from something?"

"I'm a Cenobite."

His eyes lit up. "Of course! I love it! Super sexy."

"Why thank you, my dear."

I recognized him from around town. I'd seen him in another three-piece suit at the Seattle Erotic Art Festival. He was a sub boy posing with a leather daddy for a figure-drawing workshop. I wanted him.

I drank some more and spoke over the music of the Halloween party. "Are you wearing a costume, Kent?"

"No…I don't really like costumes. I don't usually go to Cock Pit parties. Not my scene, but Ian invited me. I came here from work. I sell menswear."

I wanted to kiss him, but I didn't want to get my white foundation or gooey fake blood on his beautiful suit. We continued to do our verbal dance.

"So how do you know Ian?" I asked him. Seven-foot-tall drag queens dressed as jellyfish swayed through the crowd and brushed us with their tendrils.

"Oh, we're besties. We used to date. How do you know Ian?"

"Just from Cock Pit parties. I don't really know him well."

"Them. Ian's pronoun is 'them.' They get pretty mad if you misgender them."

"Good to know."

Kent and I stared at each other silently for a moment. Was this happening? Yes. This was happening. I kissed him. I didn't stop kissing him for a long while.

"Hello! I'm right here!" Ian butted in.

Kent and I separated. I told Ian, "Be a grown up and go seduce someone. We're making out." Ian huffed off. I went back to smooching Kent.

This went on for a bit. Eventually I pulled away. I found a napkin and cleaned the blood and makeup out of his neatly trimmed little beard.

"Do you want to dance?" I asked.

"Not really."

"Do you want to come home with me?"

"That sounds much better."

We said our goodbyes to the light.

We walked north on Broadway. "I suppose I should tell you," Kent began. He didn't make eye contact. "I'm poz and undetectable."

The night was cold and damp on my bare shoulders and chest. What a pair we made, turning the corner onto Pine Street and making our way to my car— Kent in his smart suit and I, a bloodied, blanched, black vinyl phantom.

"I'm okay with that," I told him. "Thank you for letting me know."

We intercepted my car in the parking lot of Hugo House, Seattle's literary community center. There was almost always parking on the property at night if one got there at the right time. Hugo House has since moved, and as I write this, the building (a haunted former funeral home) is a pile of splintered timber. The parking lot is torn up, tilled concrete. The homeless used to camp there overnight. So it goes in Seattle.

In the trip back to my Green Lake neighborhood, we made the small talk of those about to screw. He told me about his "three-quarter boyfriend," who lived in Mexico three or four months of the year for his fibromyalgia, escaping the exacerbating effect of the Pacific Northwest damp and cold. They were poly and open. It worked for them.

We got back to my place, where he delighted in meeting my enormous greyhound, Dorian. I didn't feel like having sex in horror drag, though that might have delighted Kent. He has a diverse sexual portfolio. I invited him to shower with me. As the makeup disappeared, he looked pleased with the man underneath.

"Is it okay if we don't fuck tonight?" I asked as we both toweled off. "I like to save that for boyfriends. I definitely want to get off with you though."

"Sure. Whatever." He didn't sound disappointed.

So we went at it. Did the usual, and as I recall a bit of the unusual. Nothing life changing. The sun was coming up when we were done. "Thanks, Kent. I really needed that."

"You're welcome. I throw a mean fuck, too."

He actually said that.

I put Dorian on his leash and the three of us walked to a Car2Go a few blocks away. I sent Kent home with a kiss and a "see you around."

I forget which one of us contacted the other first, but a week later we were hanging out again. He came over and we drove to pick up takeout.

"So," Kent asked in the car, "what did you want to do tonight?"

"Well…I was hoping we'd have sex again."

He laughed. "Yes! I really like that about you. You're so direct."

Actually, I was *practicing* being direct. As bold as I am, I have a lingering fear of crossing an unstated boundary or making someone feel deeply uncomfortable through flirting and sex talk.

Kent continued. "Of course we're going to have sex again. Anything else?"

"I dunno. Slasher movie and chill?"

"Sounds great to me. Wanna smoke some weed?"

"Fuck yeah!"

Thus we set the narrative pattern for the Kent & Evan Show. It quickly became routine for us to hang out at my house on a Tuesday night, get takeout, get stoned, watch a Dario Argento movie, and then fuck like bunnies. We even figured out how to predict the films. As we watched *Opera*, one of my favorite Argento films, the obvious protagonist casually opened a door early in the film and gasped to see a man lingering in the doorframe.

"Oh hello, the Murderer!" Kent said, and we both cracked up. By act three, the character was indeed revealed to be the murderer du jour.

I learned more about Kent. He learned more about me. The relationship grew from casual sex to closer friends. He ended up spending the night frequently. I don't recall being bothered or even particularly wary about his HIV. We joked openly about it. We both have ghoulish and politically incorrect senses of humor, which I've decided to restrain a little bit for this book (know your audience, kids). Some humor is best shared among friends.

Kent doesn't know from whom he contracted HIV. He happened to be dating an HIV-positive guy at the time, but he's sure he contracted it someplace else. Shit happens. A bathhouse, a sex party, a date—it doesn't matter where Kent got HIV. Kent prefers condomless sex, which is his right as a human being to practice. If PrEP were available earlier, I doubt he'd have HIV right now.

I continued dating other people. I remember telling my friend Yukio that I didn't want Kent to be my boyfriend. It turned out I was not dating Yukio, even though it looked a lot like dating from where I was sitting. Text messages from him said, "I had a great time tonight! Looking forward to next time!" so I suppose that's just how some people make friends. Whatever.

"I do *not* want him to be my boyfriend," I repeated while Yukio massaged me in my bed. #JustFriends.

"You're so funny. So emphatic about that." Yukio traced my spine.

"Well, I think he'd make a pretty good boyfriend if he didn't already have one. I just don't feel like sharing that much. Fuck buddies, sure, whatever. But if I'm going to buy the condo, I don't wanna do a timeshare. Just me. Plus I don't know if I can keep up with his kinks. He's really fucking kinky."

True that. Also, Kent snores. Like, holy shit does he snore. I don't know why I hate snoring so much, but it's been something I could barely deal with in previous relationships. I remember being up in the middle of the night staring at Thomas while he snored, and I would poke him till he shifted position and started breathing tolerably again. Now, I just make sure I have earplugs handy for any overnight kit. I pick my battles. I realized one day that I was more bothered by Kent snoring than his having HIV.

Kent and I kept seeing each other. The sex tiptoed more into the arena of power play. I default to pretty vanilla, and I like to get kinky and try new things, but there are some things that freak me out. As the relationship with Kent evolved, I was preparing to go into step four of my recovery process. Step four involves taking "inventory" of one's self. Each person can do it in their own way, and I went through a review of everything that I was still resentful about, ashamed of, and scared of, including how I participate in each. A lot of people drop out of the program during step four. It's a time when we discover how complicit we are in our own miseries, and what a shit we've been to other people. I recommend the experience to anyone.

My sponsor had warned me that if I wanted to get the most out of the fourth step practices, I should avoid dating and sex during that time. I had tried to do step four a couple of times, but I had to go back to step three each time. In fact, I'd been in recovery for over two years when I finally felt right to move from three to four. Step three involves surrendering control to a Higher Power (which doesn't need to be a "god" in the popular sense). That control is surrendered in order to tackle the fourth step with enough confidence that something more powerful than you (God, your community, karma, the world-soul) will help you get through it. Atheists often find Higher Power in their community, family, etc. I got far more in touch with my Paganism during step three. I began reading my Tarot twice a day as a form of prayer and request for guidance.

I suppose I was waiting for the right sign that I was ready to begin step four. That sign came in the form of sex with Kent. It was subtle, a general disquiet around the hookup. Kent snored next to me afterward, and I couldn't sleep. I tried reading, but it didn't help. I smoked some pot. Didn't help.

At about four a.m., I got out of bed again. Kent woke up this time.

"What's up?" he asked.

"Can't sleep. Not sure why."

"Huh. Do you need something?"

"I think I need to be alone. I want take you home. To your home."

I did. It was very uncomfortable.

I went through steps four and five over the next month and a half. 2013 became 2014. My sponsor suggested that giving myself a deadline to complete the step work would be very helpful, both in inspiring me to get it done and to prevent me collapsing into self-criticism. The point wasn't to create new shame. The point was to acknowledge what causes me distress and get it out of my head and down on paper, where it's less powerful.

I restrained myself from dating and hooking up. Since I'd gone long stretches without doing either in the past, I gave myself the added challenge of no flirting. That would be truly difficult for me, but worth conserving the emotional energy. I told Kent that I needed to take a break from seeing him and talking with him for about a month, and that I'd contact him when I was ready to see him again. He reluctantly agreed. He is, at base, my friend. Real friends don't coerce each other, especially kinky friends.

When my fourth and fifth step work was concluded (the fifth being an act that finishes off the work done in the fourth), I called him up.

"Hey. I'm back from the Underworld."

"Yeah? Welcome home. Did you bring me back a souvenir?"

"Of what? My emotional pain?"

Kent hesitated on the other end. "Well, it's good to hear from you. I've missed you. A lot."

"Thanks. Wanna hang out?"

"Yes. I do."

I don't recall what we did, but I know it didn't involve hooking up. His boyfriend was still in Mexico, and I assumed Kent was having sex whenever he wanted, as a handsome and street-savvy fellow like Kent can do. We kept up our friendship, but we didn't go for anything physical—at first.

A couple months later, during my visit to Everett, we talked about my sex life. "You know, I actually miss hooking up with Kent."

Everett was, as always, gentle and encouraging. "I can see why. He's handsome and hilarious. I really enjoyed meeting him at your birthday. You two make quite a team."

I looked out the window at a crow shuffling along a power line. "I wonder if

I could start hooking up with him again."

Everett perked up, inspired. "Why not?"

"Well, I pushed him away last time. He didn't enjoy that at all, but he let it happen. He was respectful of my needs."

Everett smiled. "That sounds like an excellent quality in a lover."

The crow flew away. "Ugh, but I got really weirded out and triggered last time. What if that happens again?"

"It might. But you learned a hell of a lot about yourself in step four. You have some new boundaries, and you've dropped other concerns that you don't need anymore."

Everett was making a lot of sense, and not just because I was boned up for Kent. "But Kent is so kinky. And he's poly."

"Even better. Guys who are that kinky, and especially guys in open relationships, have to navigate a lot of boundaries and be mature about them. I bet Kent is actually better at dealing with boundaries than you are at this point. He's better at it than you suspect, at least."

I waited to get home before calling him.

"Hey-girl-hey," Kent answered. "What's going on?"

"Just wrapped up a session with Everett."

"Oh yeah? How was that?"

"It was good. I figured some things out. I think I'd like to start having sex with you again."

I could picture Kent's face, his look of surprise and pensiveness that I often mistake for irritation. "Okay, we can talk about that. I'd like to have that conversation in person."

When we met up, Kent expressed his own needs and boundaries. "I was really disappointed when you told me you wanted to stop hooking up. Do you think you'll do that again?"

He made a fair point. I hadn't realized how much my little tomcat would miss his buddy. "Kent, I can't guarantee anything. That could happen. I don't know. But I want to try again now that I have some new emotional clarity and confidence. I feel different. I don't know how different, but different enough to try again."

We started over in the bedroom. It was marvelous. I even got to top him a few times, and he didn't object to me wearing condoms. I hadn't topped someone since Brandon, three years prior. Something about the tragic and shady implosion of a relationship—three days after we declared our care for each other and had intercourse for the first time—had left me once again cautious about who I'd top and under what circumstances. Being the top with Kent, having completed the most difficult period of my recovery, made me feel like sex wasn't as big a deal as I'd always made it out to be.

Kent was the first guy I slept with who used poppers in bed. I never cared for those myself, but Kent got really into them. He is definitely a champion bottom, and I was very impressed by that. Unlike my previous lovers, there was no grace period of slow adjustment while his body adjusted around me. I was on my back and he just sat right down on it like capping a marker. Bravo.

The sexual friendship felt more equal this time around; I spent time at his place frequently. The first time around, we'd mostly just hang at my place. We also got out more. Fewer slasher-movie-and-bone nights, more visits to the bars like Diesel or Pony or wherever. Could've been the weather. Could've been the natural course of the relationship.

At some point, I realized I had serious feelings for Kent. I recalled how I told Yukio that I definitely didn't want Kent to be my boyfriend. I started thinking otherwise. That was a big breakthrough for me. The affair with Nick had been a pleasant warm-up, but now I was feeling genuine budding love for an HIV-positive man for the first time, and it was like feeling it for any other man. I didn't really stop to think, *Oh wow, I think I love a poz guy! Hooty-hoot! What would mama say?*

It simply was what it was. I started thinking that perhaps I could do a poly relationship. Would it really be so bad to share my special someone with another boyfriend, while all of us also got some tail here and there on the side? One thing I knew was that I did not want to join Kent and his boyfriend in a triad. The boyfriend was not my type.

I brought up the topic stealthily one night. Perhaps I wasn't stealthy at all, who knows. I mentioned something about telling my friends about "seeing" Kent.

"You told your friends we're seeing each other?"

"Well, yeah. We hang out at least once a week and have sex. I didn't say you're my boyfriend. I just said we're 'seeing' each other."

"So you think we're dating?"

I got defensive. "Isn't 'seeing' different than 'dating?' Like a precursor to 'dating?' Isn't hooking up on the regular 'seeing' each other? I honestly never know what the fuck all these niggling little terms mean. I know we aren't boyfriends."

Truth be told: no one actually knows what these terms mean. They mean different things to different people and in different situations. The difference between "seeing" and "dating" is like the difference between ravens and crows. I know there are differences, but I can't tell them apart on sight, and they both taste like chicken to me.

Kent said, "Evan, I can't date anyone right now. That would require conversations with my partner that I don't want to have." We left it at that.

This was the beginning of the end of the sexual component of our relationship. I chose to push things a little in the direction I was feeling. Kent pushed back. That was enough for me to know that he would not make a suitable boyfriend. I became less interested in sex with him. We stayed close, but sex became less and less frequent until it evaporated entirely. We've since become best friends.

I had been thinking about getting on this newfangled "PrEP" stuff I'd just started hearing about, mostly on Scruff. Apparently it was like the Pill, but for HIV. Could that be real? If it were real, why wasn't it front page news?

Whether Kent and I continued being lovers or not, I wanted to get that protection against HIV. The last time Kent and I were at all sexual with one another, he surprised me with a spontaneous handjob while we watched *Re-Animator*. "I just wanted to play with it," he told me. That was a strange little experience.

EVAN J. PETERSON

Seven

Interlude
(Waking Up)

30 tablets

R only

THE NIGHTMARES CAME and went for a few months. I don't know how many dreams; I had at least three, perhaps many more that my sleeping brain absorbed and didn't convert to waking memory.

As I recall, they didn't begin until two or three months into my PrEP regimen. Once they did, they distressed the hell out of me. The ones that made it out of my hippocampus were disparate, but they all followed the same basic pattern:

I'm with others. Sometimes they're friends, sometimes a doctor or a nurse. I receive the news I'd dreaded for years before getting on PrEP: *Your test came back positive. You have HIV.*

In these dreams, I've been on Truvada long enough to have that 99% effectiveness rate. I panic.

But I was safe—I don't even have much anal sex—I'm always the top—I always use a condom—How is this possible?

In dreams, all is possible. Things don't behave the way I expect them to. In dreams, I see written words, but I can't read them, and it's like being suddenly struck with dyslexia or some aphasia. I can't read what the doctor wrote down, or what's on my computer screen in my test results, but I know it means I'm HIV-positive.

Sometimes I think, *Ah! I bet I'm dreaming. Wake up, Evan.* But dreams are tricky. Sometimes I get caught in a dream loop, a series of scenes in which I realize I'm dreaming and I wake up, even get out of bed, but I'm still in the dream. It's like the curse that Neil Gaiman's *Sandman*, Morpheus, inflicts upon those who've crossed him. They're doomed to eternal waking, only able to wake up inside yet another nightmare.

In dreams, there's an oversimplification of symbols, or else a confusion of them. The certainty of my recurring PrEP nightmares is that, despite my best efforts, despite religious swallowing of daily Truvada and using condoms and cutting down other risk factors, I still end up HIV-positive. The panic leads to a desperate inventory of the past few months, trying to figure out what went wrong.

Did I forget to take it one day, or several days in a row? Who did I have sex with recently? Did I somehow have unprotected sex and not even remember it? Was I drugged and raped? Did I step on a dirty syringe? Did I check a pay-phone coin return and get pricked by a trap needle?

After I wake up into this external world and not just another dream, the feeling of panic and desperation lingers for a few minutes, coupled with that sense of being responsible for my own blunder. Don't most people feel this after a particularly emotional dream?

As my friend Anthony, a psychotherapist, says about the content of dreams, "Your Superego isn't there to lecture your Unconscious." My Superego is one version of myself, a story of who I'm supposed to be. My Unconscious, however, can't give half a shit about that story.

I don't know how much waking life feeds into our dreams, or for that matter how much our dreams steer our conscious choices and reactions. What I do know is that dreams are both irrational and ultra-rational. Sometimes dreams make no sense at all, but sometimes they simplify everything down to yes/no, live/die, escape/suffer.

When I have a nightmare in which I've contracted HIV despite taking multiple scientifically-proven precautions, I'm not thinking about how shitty it is for me to consider HIV one of the worst things that could possibly happen to me. I'm not thinking about my poz friends who are healthy, happy, and living long lives. In nightmares, I don't stop to think that my health is protected by insurance, and that I should be grateful for my middle-class advantages.

In real life, HIV and its treatments are remarkably less destructive than they were thirty years ago. In real life, people with access to proper health care are rarely collapsing into gaunt, lesion-ridded victims right in front of us. In real life, people aren't burying half their friends and praying that the plague won't get them, and American children aren't contracting HIV from blood transfusions.

My unconscious doesn't live in "real" life. My unconscious is a horny, judgmental, nervous teenager with a churning imagination. Thank goodness she doesn't have a credit card. This is why I don't take Ambien.

The payoff of the nightmares is in what I can learn and how I can grow more resilient. The PrEP-failure terrors teach me that I am indeed still affected by the common fears that people blast onto the internet. That cultural paranoia remains with me, albeit overpowered by the optimistic, rational, and informed sections of my mind. While I can articulate the scientific facts, the successful studies, and all the people I've met who haven't contracted HIV since getting on PrEP—even after dropping other forms of precaution—I know that deep in my childlike unconscious mind, I'm still banging my head to Marilyn Manson songs and fearing that sex will kill me.

That's what we're really talking about here: the lingering, widespread fears that HIV is the same thing as AIDS, that HIV is inevitably deadly, and that unprotected sex will kill us. Even failed attempts at protected sex will kill us. A condom breaks, a bitten lip or canker sore creates an open wound in the mouth, and your clock begins to tick.

The gay community has to grow up at this point. I can't speak for straight people here. They have their own way of working out HIV, which varies further along racial and economic lines. But I can speak for gay dudes, at least for the middle class with healthcare access: we have to grow up when it comes to PrEP and HIV.

Our emerging culture found the opportunity to grow up when the virus first became understood, and we did grow up some. We were forced to look out for one another, to advocate for one another, to have uncomfortable conversations that would help and protect one another. We sacrificed some immediate gratification and comfort for the greater good, individually and as a community.

Maybe we stopped there. Maybe we backslid, made mistakes, got frustrated. Maybe we stopped using condoms, started again, figured out whether we wanted monogamy, polyamory, abstinence, open relationships, or orgies. The older generation of queers did a great job of keeping the community strong through the trauma. Gay culture across the world grew up a lot. Now, we need to keep growing.

America, as a nation, had to grow up after September 11th. Our tumultuous cultural adolescence of the twentieth century resulted in a wariness of authority and conformity. September 11th, however, meant another national growing-up was needed. Like a recently legal adult going off to college and getting blindsided by a sexual assault, the collective psyche of our culture needed to deal with this trauma and figure out what kind of culture to be in the aftermath. Clearly, we're still working on this: war, racism, and doomsday cults are as old as human tribes, but we've found new ways to keep them fresh and glamorous since 9/11.

The international gay community, on the other hand, already went through our personalized September 11th, but it lasted twenty years. This applies to the rest of the queer community as well: even though lesbians weren't contracting HIV at anywhere near the rate of men who have sex with men, lesbians still buried their friends and dealt with the homophobic fallout of AIDS. Trans and bisexual folks can fall into all the previous categories and more; don't fail to recognize them or the fact that trans people often get the worst of whatever's directed at the gay community, whether they're gay or not. Even through all of this, our shared community has survived and flourished.

In the past few years, more and more queer people in the world have received the human rights of marriage, health care, and safer schools. Queer and trans people are showing up more and more often in the media, but less and less often as villains, clowns, and victims.

Now, we have Truvada. Instead of a tragedy that necessitates maturity, the gay community is now facing an opportunity to keep growing up after a scientific breakthrough. Straight people went through this with the birth control pill. We're going through it with PrEP.

I don't want to live in an adolescent world of fears about what will happen if I have sex. I want to live in the reality of information, education, and confident decisions. I want to live here, now, where I have every advantage to prevent HIV while still having healthy, intimate relationships. We're finally there.

Eight

How I Learned
To PrEP

30 tablets

Rx only

RIGHT AROUND THE time things with Kent went wholly platonic, I began the process of getting on PrEP. This was a bit ironic because I started investigating PrEP so that I could be more sexually active with Kent. One big reason I even qualified for a prescription was because I had a regular poz sex partner. But let's go back a few months.

In February 2014, nearly my thirty-second birthday, I met a man named Ernie on Scruff. He was a registered nurse working at a local hospital, and his profile stated that he was on PrEP.

I must've heard about PrEP previously. People had said it was a thing that was on the way, but they said that about an HIV vaccine, too. The HIV vaccine seems like a jet pack or flying car at this point, something that we all wanted and finally got over wanting because it never became available, and besides, a jet pack could explode and kill us or give us autism or something else superstitious like that.

Why wasn't the news of PrEP everywhere? I would've surely heard about this on Facebook, right? Had I somehow missed hearing about the medical breakthrough of the twenty-first century?

I asked Ernie about it on Scruff. We eventually took the conversation off Scruff and brought it to text messages, where there would be fewer, ahem, distractions.

EJP: *So what's PrEP, exactly?*

Ernie: *It's a new treatment to prevent HIV. It stands for Pre-Exposure Prophylaxis. You take a pill every day and it's super effective at blocking HIV transmission.*

EJP: *How is that possible? I mean, of course it's possible, but why aren't more people talking about it?*

Ernie: *I don't know. It's weird how few people are talking about it. The clinical trials show it to be incredibly reliable.*

EJP: *Huh. Is it expensive?*

Ernie: *Can be. Depends on your insurance. Gilead, the company that makes it, offers a reduced or free copay if you apply for it. That's what I use.*

EJP: *I'm on Group Health right now.*

Ernie: *I think that one is like $30-40 copay, but don't quote me on that. The state of Washington also offers a drug assistance option.*

EJP: *That seems pretty cheap.*

Ernie: *You can get a prescription if you fall in certain demographics. If you have a poz partner or you've had an STI in the last year.*

EJP: *I do have a poz fwb. Thank you for telling me all of this.*

Ernie:	*Hey, my pleasure. I want people to know what their options are. I feel like the more of us talk about it, the more people will be safer.*
EJP:	*You sound like a great guy. Want to meet up sometime?*
Ernie:	*Totally! How does this week look for you?*

Ernie and I went on a date to the Backdoor Lounge. No, it's not a gay bar. The title is a single entendre. Ernie was just as handsome in person as in his pics. He was a bit older than me, maybe around forty. In the low and flickering light of the lounge, we ate and drank and talked of spirituality and PrEP and gay stuff. We talked about his shaved head. I reached up and rubbed it gently, a move I wouldn't usually do across a table in a restaurant, but I was feeling bold, and I was definitely into Ernie.

A few minutes later, I went in for the kill: I took off my glasses. I'm not sure what magical geometry changes in my face when I take off my glasses, but the fellas report that my eyes become a lot more powerful. I'm like Cyclops from the X-Men, except nothing like him.

In the parking lot, I wanted to kiss Ernie, but I didn't. I don't even know why I didn't. Sometimes I don't know what to do. We reluctantly parted ways.

He texted me a few minutes later.

Ernie:	*Thanks for a great time!*
EJP:	*Thank YOU, Ernie! I really wanted to kiss you, but I wasn't sure if you wanted that…*
Ernie:	*Oh man, absolutely! Why didn't we kiss?*
EJP:	*I dunno. Let's make out next time. Want to meet up again this week?*

I went over to his place two nights later. He prepared a homemade pasta, and I brought the salad. His bookshelves were lined with various new age volumes. I found out he'd been Mormon once, and he had even been married and had kids before realizing that he couldn't pretend to be straight anymore. He told me he had a great relationship with his kids. Pictures of the children were up around the apartment. My duderus quivered.

We talked more about PrEP. He told me that some people have stomach trouble on it, but it usually doesn't last. He told me that, for him, it was totally worth being on it. It sounded like a miraculous drug. No, not miraculous; miracles are about magic and faith and the supernatural. It sounded like science fiction, but it was happening, just like touch-screen computers and Facetime and Pokemon Go. The big difference of course was that unlike a touch-screen computer that fits in your pocket, PrEP wasn't being talked about casually on TV (yet), and people weren't using it everywhere you looked.

After dinner, we cuddled up on the couch. He said he wanted to "share energy" with me, however that happened. I was pretty sure how it was going to happen. Sex was an option, but not something he pushed for. So we shared our energy. We cuddled. We kissed. We watched the remake of *Steel Magnolias*—the version starring Queen Latifah, Jill Scott, and Phylicia Rashad. Then, of course, we went upstairs to his bedroom.

When my PrEP article came out in *The Stranger* in November 2014[1], I sent him the link and thanked him for his guidance in helping me understand PrEP. He posted the link on Facebook, and he accompanied it with a statement about how much it means to know he made a difference. He certainly did; this book you're reading is in part a result of one person putting a reference to PrEP in his Scruff profile and welcoming any reader to ask him questions about it. It started there for me.

To GET CLEARED for a PrEP prescription, I had to show a negative HIV test, so I went and got my usual test regimen. Everything checked out, but that was almost a month before I finally got the pills into my hands. I had a few sexual encounters during that time, and I wanted to get tested once more. My new

HIV specialist, Dr. Kathy Brown, agreed that I could do so.

I thought about my first HIV/STD test in Tallahassee, Florida. The trepidation of getting an HIV test, followed by the relief of a negative result, has faded over the years. It's become a routine. There's always a faint and ominous shimmer of what-if, but in general I just go in, get needled, and then go grab a chai.

A few days after starting my Truvada, I received the results of my latest HIV test. I thought about how I've come so far, been diligent about condoms, and had the recommended conversations with new partners. If I were to test positive now, on the verge of being possibly impervious to HIV? That would be a bitter irony.

I clicked the "lab results" link on my Group Health online profile. My HIV test: negative.

I cried.

Soon, I was having cake brunch at Cupcake Royale with Christopher Frizzelle, then-Editor-in-Chief of *The Stranger*, one of Seattle's alternative newspapers. I had written one article for him, but my pitches hadn't landed since then. Now, Christopher was excitedly handing me the PrEP assignment I'd pitched via email. We even met in person to work out the details. I felt honored, respected, and inspired to do the best I could.

We went over things like bathhouses (nope, I've never been to one), crystal meth (never touch the stuff), the growing buzz around PrEP on the apps, and what he expected and required for this essay to be published in *The Stranger*. He even gave me a 5000-word goal, which is an extraordinary amount of space in print.

On my way out, I met and chatted up Trent, the adorable barista. We hooked up a few times afterward. Hi, Trent!

In between whiling away the hours with Trent and Kent and Brent and the other members of the boy band that populated my bed that summer, I got down to the business of interviewing guys in person and online. I signed up for Facebook groups like #TruvadaWhore, which is actually about eliminating the stigma against guys on PrEP, whether they're promiscuous or not. Here are some of the things I learned in interviews.

My buddy Scott, a mid-thirties shamanic practitioner who does something boring for the corporate sector during the day, told me that his behavior shifted significantly since getting on PrEP a year before. Scott told me that he initially had fewer sexual partners than usual once he got onto PrEP, but then the number went up. He also started having unprotected sex with other guys on PrEP and undetectable poz partners.

Over brunch at a precious little diner, he told me, "There's another level of okayness with having a long-term, HIV-positive partner that wasn't there before."

Scott, as adventurous and open about sexuality as he is with friends, didn't want his last name to be used in my journalism. Scott has concerns about social stigma toward himself as well as his partners that may result from being publicly identified as being on PrEP and having unprotected sex. This was common among those I interviewed, a result of the culture of judgment and finger-pointing, especially within the gay community, about our individual sexual decisions. It's crazy to me that the fingers pointed at us in shame come primarily from other gay men. Straight people don't even realize PrEP exists most of the time.

There are certainly exceptions to that, including straight people on the drug regimen. I've had some trouble finding them for interviews, whereas many queer men have been all too happy to talk about it, but straight people on preventative Truvada certainly exist. Notably, I've also had trouble finding trans women on PrEP to talk to, but this may all relate to where I'm looking for potential interviewees (Facebook, primarily, including the PrEP-interest groups).

PrEP is for everyone, it's just obviously more discussed among gay/queer men. "Kelly," a woman I met through a Facebook group, is a heterosexual woman in a relationship with an HIV-positive straight man. She told me that her partner contracted HIV from his ex-wife, who didn't know she had HIV, and she in turn contracted it from her previous partner, who used IV drugs. Kelly had been with her boyfriend for ten months when I interviewed her in fall 2016, and she had been on PrEP for three months. Kelly uses PrEP to stay safe with her partner and for both of their peace of mind. She told me that he was very afraid of transmitting HIV to her, more afraid that she was, especially because he's undetectable. Now that she's on PrEP, things in their relationship have improved a lot. They do not use condoms, which Kelly told me she'd only used for birth control previous to this relationship.

There are lots of people like Kelly and her partner out there. Straight couples, monogamous couples, people who don't fit the stereotypical image of AIDS and HIV.

Several of my friends have not minded providing their full names. Stephen Mills, a poet and author in his thirties living in New York City, told me that he and his partner continue to make the same choices they did before getting on PrEP, but he likes knowing that he has extra protection. He and his partner had an open relationship at the time I interviewed him (summer 2014), but that started long before they got on Truvada. They continued to use condoms for casual partners but not with one another.

"It provides a safety net if there are ever any slip-ups," Stephen told me. He and his partner pay for PrEP with their insurance, and then Gilead's own assistance program covers the remainder of the cost. Stephen has experienced no side effects.

Like me, Stephen feels called to be a PrEP activist, especially as a writer. He's been "extremely disappointed in many members of the gay community" who have "spread completely untrue and unfounded claims." He, like many of the people I interviewed, did his research carefully. "We have to educate people… We've been telling people to use condoms for years, and it hasn't completely worked, so why not offer something else?"

Adam Zeboski, an HIV testing counselor at the San Francisco AIDS Foundation, has been the leader and poster boy of the #TruvadaWhore campaign. He reclaimed the term "Truvada whore" and made it a hashtag meme when an HIV-positive journalist, David Duran, used it as a way of denouncing perceived-risky choices while on PrEP. Duran has since changed his mind, and Zeboski told me that he and Duran have since, ahem, "reconciled."

Zeboski began following me on Twitter and favoriting my #PrEP posts the day I began tweeting my daily side effects or lack thereof. I joined his #TruvadaWhore group on Facebook and began talking to other guys about their experiences.

According to Zeboski: "I've only had amazing side effects, like no more anxiety about sex, more fun, more intimacy, more connection, better relationships, etc.," His condom use is inconsistent, but he believes that condomless sex on PrEP is safer sex. I tend to agree.

Roger, a sixty-year-old queer (not "gay," but queer) Seattle man in a same-sex marriage, told me that he did have mild digestive discomfort for the first two weeks, but that these symptoms quickly abated. His partner is HIV-positive and he is not.

"Had this pill come along in 1984, or 1994," Roger told me, "many of our friends and lovers would have taken it in a second, and would be here with us today... Given that, the rest of the debates are absurd."

Luke, a therapist working in San Francisco, told me that he found that his patients in serodiscordant relationships are likely to use PrEP now instead of condoms, which his patients considered "literal barriers to intimacy." However, this is not the case with all his clients: "Many of the patients with whom I work have been using condoms *more* since going on PrEP... Part of their strategy has also been more open discussion with partners about testing and treatment, status and viral load, etc... Most of these patients were not using condoms at all before."

One trend I noticed among nearly everyone I interviewed: they're all invested in conducting their own research and making educated choices about their sexual health. They're informed.

Eric, a gay musician in an open relationship, was happy to be interviewed, but didn't want his full name used. "There is such an odd backlash against guys on PrEP... People [have called] it the 'whore pill.'"

Eric's doctor, who is also gay, told him that guys on PrEP are actually quite likely to continue using condoms. The fact that Eric's doctor is gay is part of another pattern worth pointing out. Not only do gay people tend to prefer to have gay doctors (duh), but gay doctors tend to be more PrEP-savvy than many straight ones. Anyone who asks, "Why do you need a gay doctor?" has a lot of privilege, and that's not a term I like to throw around.

I need a gay doctor because my straight doctors have occasionally been blithering idiots when it comes to dealing with issues specific to queer patients. Dr. S. isn't the only doctor who had a shitty bedside manner when it came to discussing sexuality issues. I once went to a gastroenterologist for acid reflux, and it was interfering with my eating habits. I had lost weight and couldn't seem to put it back on.

"Are you a homosexual?" the doctor asked almost immediately. Was he serious?

"Yes. Why does that matter?" I said, already knowing what he was implying.

"Well, if you've had recent weight loss, it could be HIV."

I assured him that I get tested regularly. I never went to see him or his office partners again.

This is a very shitty question for a doctor to ask a patient. When I told him I'd had unplanned weight loss, he could simply have asked, "Have you been tested recently for HIV?" Instead, he immediately asked me if I'm a homosexual. He associated HIV with being gay, and vice versa, as opposed to a doctor familiar with the LGBTQ community, who would know better. I wasn't offended so much as shocked and dismayed that a relatively young doctor in a highly liberal city like Seattle would be so tone-deaf as to ask a patient flat-out if he's gay, thus implying that gay people are the only ones who need to be checked for HIV as opposed to any patient with unexpected weight loss. After the debacle with that gastroenterologist, I asked my insurance at the time (United Health) to match me up with a GI who is knowledgeable on LGBTQ populations.

They put me with the gayest doctor I've ever had, and I loved every moment. He was a darling. Before I went under anesthesia for an endoscopy, he squeezed my shoulder and said, "You're gonna do great!"

I don't let just anyone stick a camera down my throat. Dr. Craig, if you're reading this, I've always loved you.

Now that I'm on Group Health, the two doctors who handle my PrEP treatment are both savvy. In response to finding out that I have been dating poz guys intentionally, Dr. Brown brought up the term "sero-sorting." The term means asking one's sex partners about their HIV status and making choices accordingly. While the traditional sorting practice for HIV-negative people has been to only have sex with HIV-negative partners, and poz people to have poz partners, Brown's gay male patients are reporting the opposite. With the rise of the undetectable HIV category, contracting the virus is statistically much lower (almost impossible) risk when intentionally having sex with an undetectable poz partner, as opposed to having sex with a partner who is HIV positive but unaware of it. The latter is actually quite risky.

I am one of these new, inverse sero-sorting queer men. I feel safer having sex with someone who is poz, undetectable, and vigilant about taking his pills daily. I know exactly what my risk factors are and what to do about them. With PrEP, I now have even more peace of mind about my own body. Others' bodies are their own business.

On the subject of other people's business: I myself received a bit of judgment when I decided to post on Facebook about my choice to get on PrEP. I decided to try on the activist hat and "be the change" I want to see in the world, etc. The hat, as you may have noticed, fit.

The reactions were pretty much as expected. Most friends and family, straight and queer, conservative and liberal, were supportive and encouraging. Some made sure to remind me to "be careful," which is the well-intentioned common response when a queer man—or, for that matter, any woman—mentions that they intend to have sex.

There were three prominent responses that gave me pause. One gay acquaintance whom I never see in person felt the need to question why I would announce such a thing on Facebook. He's an asshole, which is why I don't ever see him in person. A closer friend in New York City, who tends to be Polly Pessimist in general, commented that while he supports my decision, he would never take this pill because he doesn't participate in "high-risk activities." This seems rather self-righteous and not-so-subtly prejudiced against poz people.

The thing is that I *do* participate in "high-risk activities," since protected sex with HIV-positive people is still commonly considered "high risk."

Several middle-aged friends and family, survivors of the AIDS crisis, cautioned me to be wary of side effects. The generation that came before me is still reeling from the nasty complications of AZT and the other early treatments, but they supported my decision. Except, of course, for my aunt.

She helped raise me, instilling values I stand up for, including my decision to become an activist for PrEP. She told me, fearfully and without hesitation, that HIV does not cause AIDS—that AIDS is a hoax to sell pills and kill gays.

My aunt's trepidation is compassionate. She saw several of her gay friends suffer terribly on AZT in the early days of treatment. AZT was an incredibly harsh treatment, and I encourage you to do your own research on it. One of my aunt's friends was prescribed AZT by a doctor who never even tested him; knowing that the man had a same-sex partner who had HIV was enough for this doctor to advise him to get on AZT. My aunt is convinced that it's AZT that killed this man, not the HIV that he was never even tested for.

My aunt cares passionately about marginalized people, gays in particular, and she loves my sister and me as the children she never had. It is a mother's heart from which she begged me not to take HIV drugs.

When I was about eighteen and becoming sexually active, she sent me a book called *What If Everything You Thought You Knew About AIDS Was Wrong*, written by Christine Maggiore. Maggiore wrote somewhat convincingly that HIV is a harmless virus, known as a "passenger virus," while AIDS is actually the result of drug abuse and other diseases that result in a severely weakened immune system. All of this information (and misinformation) is now readily available on the internet.

This was definitely food for thought to my impressionable young mind, but not enough to convince me to stop worrying about HIV. I'm glad I didn't get on that bandwagon. Maggiore died of what the Los Angeles Times reported as pneumonia[2], which is often a major AIDS-defining illness. Other sources[3] claim her death certificate makes it clear she died of herpes infection combined with long-term pneumonia, which would also be AIDS-defining illnesses, the kind that only kill people with severely repressed immune systems. For accountability, I must point out that I have not seen Maggiore's death certificate, nor can I find it in the online articles and blog that supposedly link to it.

I believe Christine Maggiore was wrong. I believe she died from the complications of AIDS, which she developed as a result of being HIV-positive. Her HIV-positive toddler, Eliza Jane, died of pneumocystis pneumonia, which was better documented. That form of pneumonia is a specific AIDS-defining illness.

My aunt called and left a long voicemail cautioning me not to take Truvada, that she'd read the side effects online and was seriously spooked. She asked me to call her as soon as I could. I didn't want to. I didn't know what to say. Within a few days, even my mother was calling to ask if I'd talked to my aunt yet. I thought this happens in every family, but it doesn't. Some families all talk about who is in conflict with whom and what to do about it. Other families just leave people alone to work that out between them. My family is a "this person said this to that person, and I heard it from so-and-so, but I wasn't supposed to tell you that, so don't repeat it, even if you're upset and want to discuss it with the person who originally said it" kind of family, except for my dad, who just wants chill and figure out what he's making for dinner.

Finally, I called my aunt back. It was about eight days later. My aunt told me that she is completely convinced that HIV doesn't cause AIDS. In the '90s, she'd done her own research, reading books like Peter Duesberg's *Inventing the AIDS Virus*. At that time, HIV couldn't be made to fulfill Koch's postulates, which she told me were the "gold standard" of defining a disease. Koch's postulates are criteria developed to establish the relationship between disease conditions and the organisms that cause them.

Over the phone, we had a tough conversation.

"Evan, did I ever give you that book, *What If Everything You Thought You Knew About AIDS Was Wrong?*"

"Yes, and I read it avidly cover to cover. And that was fifteen years ago. Things have changed. The medications are much safer, and people who would've died by now are still alive. Did you know Maggiore died of AIDS? That her three year old died of AIDS?"

I was getting upset.

"Evan, I'm telling you, AIDS isn't caused by HIV."

"I need to do my own research on that. Auntie, we may need to just agree to disagree on this. I believe HIV causes AIDS. I do not want to get HIV. That's why I'm going on PrEP."

She pressed the issue. "What about condoms? What's wrong with using condoms if you're concerned about HIV?"

"I do use condoms, Auntie, but I rarely have anal sex. Condoms aren't foolproof, either. You know I get canker sores in my mouth. Usually, they're very bad and they can last for two weeks. I want to be able to have oral sex without worrying about that."

Then she crossed the last line I could tolerate. "So don't have oral sex!"

"That is simply not going to happen. I'm not going to switch from oral sex to anal sex just so I can use condoms more often."

"Well, why don't you just try to have a monogamous partner?"

By this point I was crying. "I *tried* to have a monogamous partner for the last fifteen years, and that just resulted in a lot of disappointment and heartache. I had to go into twelve-step recovery because I was trying so hard to have a monogamous partner. I've never been in a long-term relationship, and I'm done trying to make that happen. Maybe, once I start dating more HIV-positive guys, it'll finally happen."

The conversation was not going anywhere because my aunt and I live in two different realities. She lives in a reality in which HIV does not cause AIDS. I live in a reality in which HIV is widespread, and it usually develops into AIDS if it's not treated with medication, and AIDS is usually an agonizing way to die.

You cannot have a successful debate between two people who live in different realities. It's the same reason why atheists and fundamentalists cannot have a debate that results in a win for either side. Atheists live in a reality in which their beliefs are completely supported. So do fundamentalists, but that's a very different reality. Reality is what you believe, no matter how daffy that may be. See also: Facebook.

My aunt asked me to promise her that I would read about Dr. Peter Duesberg, a tenured professor at UC Berkeley, who has made outstanding breakthroughs in cancer research. Unfortunately, his brilliance in one area of medicine is paired with adamant backwardness in another. He hypothesized that HIV doesn't lead to AIDS. I usually support dissent and scientific radicalism—that's how we make progress and discover breakthroughs. However, Dr. Duesberg clings tenaciously to a hypothesis that has been disproved in several ways. Christine Maggiore, it should be noted, seems to have formed her opposition to the HIV/AIDS connection soon after meeting Duesberg.

I did read up on Duesberg, and I visited his self-published website. As of this writing (late 2016), it's woefully behind on the new research into HIV and its medications. In fact, he does much more to repeatedly promote his own writing on the subject than to dismantle other clinical research into HIV. There are frequent typos, particularly in the FAQ section, which also seems particularly attached to Italian HIV studies. The FAQ section also features several logical fallacies or outright obfuscations, particularly when it talks about condoms (paraphrased: Question—Are you saying condoms are useless to prevent the spread of HIV? Answer—HIV doesn't cause AIDS. Drugs cause AIDS. Therefore, condoms are useless to prevent AIDS). The site doesn't talk much about all the drug-free people who have died of AIDS.

I've taught research methods to college students for ten years, and these issues immediately erode the trustworthiness of the information on the site. Duesberg teaches science. I teach how to detect questionable information. Feel free to look at the website yourself, if it's still there (it occasionally disappears, then reappears): www.duesberg.com.

By the way, I reached out to Dr. Duesberg with the journalistic olive branch of objectivity. He responded to my query. When I sent him questions about the rise of PrEP, he sent me back a scientific article he published with the *Italian Journal of Anatomy and Embryology*, titled "AIDS since 1984: No evidence for a new, viral epidemic—not even in Africa." That article was published in 2011, before PrEP became widely available, and the article doesn't address PrEP. Duesberg's implication is that his stance on PrEP is no different than his stance on any HIV medication, and nothing has changed in the last few years. I anticipated that, but it would've been nice to have a quote specifically about PrEP.

Even among AIDS deniers and dissidents, there's no across-the-board coherency. Some say HIV and AIDS both exist, but there's no connection between them. Others say there's no such thing as HIV to begin with. Still others say that yes, HIV exists, but AIDS isn't real, just a pattern of symptoms haphazardly associated by circumstance.

I've no doubt that Duesberg would run circles around me in a debate. He's a brilliant scientist. Despite my not being a doctor or scientist, I'm a very clever man. I know how to find information. To resolve the questions my aunt brought up, I called my ex-boyfriend Lane, a Wikipedian specializing in public health information. If anyone I trust intimately is up-to-date on his HIV knowledge, it's Lane.

He explained Koch's postulates to me and how HIV is tricky enough to require extra measures to apply these standards. It's not that HIV doesn't satisfy the postulates; we just have to take extra steps. It's like making three right turns because you can't take a left turn. You end up pointed in the correct direction eventually. This is why there's room for AIDS dissidence. Rather than drift further into the minutiae of explaining that yes, AIDS and HIV exist and they're connected, I'll let readers look it up online. See the endnotes[4] for a link to get you started.

I'm not saying AZT was the solution in the early days of AIDS. In fact, I think AZT probably did kill a lot of people who could've lived with HIV for a while longer. But things have changed. Pretend this is *Reading Rainbow*, and I'm the ever-foxy Levar Burton. You don't have to take my word for it. Please do your own reading.

It's this lingering AIDS panic and skepticism that is fueling the Truvada controversies. I talked about this in my *Stranger* article. My aunt was not pleased, and when I initially asked if she'd let me interview her for this book, she said she didn't want anything to do with this topic. Since then, I had the opportunity to spend a few days with her, and we reconciled. She was glad that I at least made the attempt to interview Duesberg. My aunt and I love each other.

I got onto PrEP anyway. I had second-guessed myself enough by then. I'd already interrogated myself about taking a potentially harmful medication. I'd already waded through the difficulty I had believing that PrEP was real. I'd already gone through the cognitive noise of a lifetime of "condoms or abstinence" conditioning. I was ready to go from "condoms or..." to "condoms and...."

EVAN J. PETERSON

Nine

Unpacking the Fudge:
An Exploration of
Anal Sex, Condoms
and Shame

30 tablets

℞ only

I WANT THIS book to be accessible to straight readers. Nonetheless, it's impossible for me to write a memoir without focusing mainly on my own experience, which is incidentally that of a gay white American man. That means condoms and butt stuff, always in stereotype and sometimes in practice.

Mainstream American culture has a strange relationship with butt sex. It's a universally understood option for people of all genders and sexualities. Straight men often fetishize the hell out of it. I remember hearing boys barely twelve years old talking in my middle school about a certain girl and how much they wanted to "fuck her in the ass." This isn't just a Florida thing, either.

Plenty of women enjoy butt sex as well. Even lesbians often like it—I know lesbians that enjoy being pegged in the butt by their partners, as well as those who like pegging their partner in the ass. For women, it seems that the mechanics of anal penetration stimulate the vagina from outside-in rather than inside-out, not to mention the vast majority of the clitoris, which we now know is mostly internal. At least, this is what my cis-female friends who enjoy anal sex have told me.

Whether you're male, female, or non-binary, whether you're straight or not, anal sex feels wonderful to many people. Straight guys have begun to experiment and talk about having their butts penetrated, at least played with, by their female partners. Butt stuff is not a gay thing. Butt stuff is for everyone! Cue shooting star spreading a rainbow behind it. *The More You Know.*

Even so, lots of gay guys don't like anal sex. I know plenty of gay guys that have sex lives based on a great variety of other options, and even gay people find this difficult to believe. I did not make ass play—my butt or my partner's—an ongoing part of my sex life until I was twenty-eight years old. Sure, I'd tried things, but I felt like I just wasn't wired to enjoy things happening to my butt. I've since changed my mind.

Not everyone gets into it, and that's okay. Take it from your buddy Evan J. Peterson, and take it hard: you are healthy if you enjoy anal sex. You are healthy if you don't enjoy anal sex.

Here's where things get more complicated. Anal sex isn't just about the sensation of objects and surfaces interacting with the outer and inner ass. A huge factor in enjoying or not enjoying anal sex is the *idea of anal sex*—the taboos, the power, the powerful and often subconscious psychological associations with the asshole.

Here's where we get into semiotics. Without getting a master's degree, you can understand the basics of a complicated and jargony field like semiotics. Semiotics, simply put, is the study and philosophy of making meaning from symbols. They don't need to be visual symbols; one concept can symbolize another concept. Case in point: the *idea* of anal sex, not to mention the practice, can symbolize pleasure, pain, male homosexuality, heterosexual kink, filth, disease, love, tenderness, connection, intimacy, rape, prison, femininity, masculinity, strength, fragility, vulnerability, power, and Greeks. There's some semiotics for you.

Anal sex means something. In fact, all sex means something, even if you claim it's NSA (No Strings Attached, not the National Security Agency). Even if you go to a bathhouse and get drilled by a succession of anonymous strangers in a pitch-black room, there is meaning and emotion attached.

People die and kill each other over sex. People will drive or fly or bus hundreds of miles to meet someone for sex. We often call that "romance" and "love," but I've never driven to another state just to cuddle. I have, on the other hand, driven to Jefferson Davis County, Georgia, to have some sex with a longtime internet flirtation. I drove three and a half hours to a county still named after the leader of the fucking Confederacy just to get laid with someone I'd fantasized about for years. Maybe it was my micro-rebellion against the socially backward norms of the South: making love to another man in Jefferson Davis County, which sounds like a great title for a country song.

This is the power of sex and what it means to people. Anal sex is but one specific way to go about it. So let's unpack the associations and meaning that we attach to it.

Here's a brief list of terms often associated with anal sex, regardless of the genders of those having it:

+ Dirty

+ Naughty

+ Nasty

+ Freaky

+ Kinky

+ Filthy

+ Weird

+ Painful

+ Gross

+ Sick

+ Weak

+ Effeminate

+ Gay

I see an across-the-board association with anal sex as something outside of "normal." Even for many gay men, anal sex isn't considered completely normal. It's a thing we do because *we aren't normal*. Sometimes, that makes it more fun. The thrill of a taboo is intoxicating. Other times, it indicates the overwhelming amount of residual guilt and shame we've been taught about being queer.

When many people think of homosexual people or hear the word "gay," the semiotics of these terms and concepts mean that people immediately think about anal sex. I've spent a very long time thinking about this, and whether I'm exaggerating and aspiring to be a mind reader. I'm now completely confident in my estimate when I assure you that millions—millions!—of people immediately think *Ass Fucking* when they are confronted with the mere idea of male homosexuality. This image association is so widespread that the word "homosexual" itself usually makes straight people think of gay men, not lesbians.

I've heard countless gay people tell me anecdotes about times that straight people—family, friends, strangers—immediately brought up sex in response to learning or detecting that they were in the presence of a homosexual. Parents can be the worst, actually. They hear that their son is gay or bisexual and one of the first things many say is, "So you want to have sex with men?" If the parent is particularly venomous in their homophobia, they'll even get explicit and crude. My friend Wylie told me that when he came out to his Southern Baptist father, he actually asked, "So you want dick in your mouth? Dick in your ass?"

This happens to lesbians and bisexual women all the time as well. Women tell me consistently that family and strangers alike will make comments about cunnilingus, strap-ons, and finger-fucking when confronted with the sudden revelation that a woman is queer. That's how powerfully being gay is associated with sex. It actually says a lot about the person making the association.

Think about all the "jokes" that you heard growing up about gay people:

"What do you call a lesbian dinosaur?" *Lickalottapuss.*

"How do you get four gay men to sit on the same barstool?" *Turn it upside down.*

"What's a common pickup line in a gay bar?" "*Can I push in your stool?*"

"Some gay guys and some lesbians live next door to each other in San Francisco, and they're all going to the beach. Who gets there first?" *The lesbians, because while they're doing sixty-nine on the highway, the gays are still home packing their shit.*

We can also see from these sorts of infantile jokes that many straight people assume that lesbian sex is all just oral sex, which I assure you it is not.

My dad actually used the upside-down barstool line on me one time, but we were half-joking and intentionally pushing one another's buttons. I think I started it, that time. He's a good dad, and way before he knew that I'm gay, he told me, "I'd rather see two men make love than see them kill each other. Love is always better than hate."

But so many parents aren't like mine, because we still live in a world (a changing one, to be sure) in which *Gay=Sex, Lust* and *Straight=Love, Marriage, Children, Family.* That's pretty unfair to straight people, too.

Tied up inextricably with assumptions and beliefs about gay sex are assumptions and beliefs about gender. When we look at the proliferation of homosexuality in ancient Greek and Roman culture (the incomplete picture we know of them from surviving fragments), homosexuality was often acceptable as long as the men stayed manly. This led to some difficult gendering issues— not the least of which was deciding how to have sex without "feminizing" either partner. There was of course a double standard: a man putting his own cock into another man's mouth or butt was okay, but having another man's cock go into him was feminizing, nasty, weak, etc. Frottage was a popular solution, which will be of interest to the frot queens reading.

This way of thinking still exists. For some men who have sex with men (abbreviated MSM in medicine, sociology, etc.), the man who puts his cock into another man's body isn't gay. The man who is penetrated is the gay one. The act of penetrating makes you a man; to be penetrated makes you something other than a man.

Gay sex is rife with stigma. With that in mind, we can understand why so many gay guys, after 30+ years of an HIV epidemic, still choose not to use condoms.

Condomless sex is commonly known as "barebacking" or "fucking raw" among gay men. Ejaculating inside your partner without a condom is known as "breeding" (I kid you not, dear straight readers). The term "breeding" does have early connotations of the semen being HIV-positive. Now, however, to get bred is just to have your partner cum inside you, regardless of their HIV status. This is an extremely popular practice, and humans probably evolved to enjoy this sharing of fluids. Some people love it. Some people are afraid of it. Some are unimpressed one way or the other.

Unfortunately, even many gay men scratch their heads and accuse one another of gross negligence when it comes to unprotected sex. That's one of the loudest objections to PrEP, believe it or not. People are afraid that the use of such an effective HIV-prevention method will lead to rampant unprotected sex.

What I've heard countless times as I've interviewed people on PrEP is this: those who have lots of condomless sex on PrEP are in general the same people who were having lots of condomless sex without PrEP. Other STIs are not a deterrent and never have been. People don't mind. Many people believe that STIs are simply part of being a sexually active adult. Many of them are curable, and they're becoming more preventable than ever.

It's also pretty easy to avoid fixing your own life and your own flaws when you're focusing on the flaws of others. Maybe this is what the Bible was talking about where it says, "Judge not, that you be not judged" (Matthew 7:1-3). I also look to Dante's *Inferno*, Canto 23, wherein the hypocrites spend eternity in hell weighed down by lead robes lacquered in gold. It's a fancy kind of damnation.

Unprotected sex has always been common and popular. Did syphilis stop straight people from getting laid outside of wedlock over the last five hundred years? Nope. Syphilis was deadly, disfiguring, and altogether horrifying, but people for centuries have had sex at the risk of catching it. Condoms and other prophylactics were accessible to many of those people, but that doesn't mean they used them. Now, aren't we lucky that syphilis is curable?

Instead of demonizing condomless sex and the folks who prefer it and practice it, what could we learn if we approached the subject without judgment? Condomless sex is no less or more than an option. Thirty years of AIDS crisis have convinced many of us that condomless sex is wrong, destructive, even malevolent. That's a huge burden for people to carry. For gay men, in addition to being told they're wrong and sick for being gay, those who prefer condomless sex are told they're wrong and sick for how they have sex, not just who they do it with. Lately, this message of wrongness and sickness comes from other gay people more often than it does from straight people. Straight people have other shit to worry about, like Zika and women's reproductive rights.

Many people do in fact stop using condoms because they're on PrEP. That's the tricky nature of data and surveys—people can tell you that blankety-blank percent of people stop using condoms after going on PrEP, but you need to know that the huge portion of that percent is made up of people who weren't consistent in condom use anyway. Similarly, the statistics about STIs being on the rise among PrEP communities need to take into account that people on PrEP are being tested for STIs more often.

Condoms are only effective if you use them, and even then, they can break. They can fall off. PrEP doesn't fall off. It's clear that PrEP is not intended to prevent the spread of other STIs. It also doesn't prevent pregnancy or the regret of waking up next to what's-their-name. But hey, it prevents the transmission of HIV, which is a huge-ass deal. AIDS is arguably the most destructive global epidemic of the last three decades.

The cure for HIV may never be found. The only "cure" we have is knowledge and technology: education, information, and prevention methods such as Truvada and condoms. Thanks to PrEP and the poz-undetectable status, prevention is now all about having sex, with abstinence merely an effective but unnecessary and out-of-style option.

That brings us back to the popular speculation that using PrEP leads to rampant promiscuity. Speaking only for myself, I have been no more or less promiscuous than I was before getting on Truvada. My dating and hookup patterns vary with the seasons, especially now that I live in Seattle, which has lately had three seasons: Lovely, Too Hot, and The Sky Weeps & So Must We. I find that I feel a lot of ease and interest in casual sex during late spring and summer. By late summer, I begin feeling that I want to settle into something monogamous with someone special. During Fallwinter (all one season here), it's hit or miss, and mostly I'm just disgruntled that so many people are passive-aggressive, aloof, and inconsistent. In the midst of those emotional patterns, my sexual behavior hasn't changed much after starting my PrEP regimen.

I certainly know guys who've had a higher number of sexual partners after getting on PrEP. I also know guys who didn't even bother to start PrEP because they have consistently low numbers of sex partners, they like to date exclusively, etc. My friend Matt, for instance, has a monogamous HIV-positive fiancée, and they feel that PrEP would be redundant while he's undetectable. While he was single, Matt refused to take Truvada because, as he put it, he distrusts the American trend of overmedicating, and he doesn't believe his sexual behaviors are risky. PrEP is not for everyone. Neither is Claritin.

I hear people keep bringing up worries that PrEP will lead to orgies. *Orgies! Good God! Call the fire department! Turn on the hoses!* Surely there's nothing worse for Americans than orgies. Not an epidemic of gun violence, not ISIS/ISIL, not childhood obesity or cancer, not people refusing to vaccinate their children and thereby spreading deadly and preventable diseases because they think vaccines are magic autism darts, not a presidential election cycle that has quickly eroded our communal sanity—

Nope! It's orgies. But people never stopped having orgies. The genders of the people who attend them and the places they're held are arbitrary. This has been going on during the entire AIDS crisis, and the world hasn't ended. HIV was curbed anyway, though not eradicated. Most HIV-positive people I know contracted it from an encounter with one partner, not from an orgy. Those who did pick up HIV in an orgy setting knew what they were doing, and many of them don't have regrets.

I've been quite delighted to hear several times from my straight friends the same basic sentiment about this fear of the PrEP orgy: "What's wrong with orgies?" Bless you all.

Recently, three different guys in a week told me the same basic insight, which surprised me: the main reasons they go to bathhouses is for the relaxed intimacy of a queer-men-only space. It's not as much about who or how many they'll hook up with; it's about being among queer men without having to tailor their behavior to the straight world. As someone who has never been to a bathhouse or an orgy (because of a lingering fear of strangers molesting me, and I'll own that fear), this was a huge revelation to me. I never understood the culture of anonymous sex parties, and that's because I'd never been to one. What I'm discovering is that they aren't all that "anonymous" much of the time.

My good friend Javier told me the following via text message. I've quoted him nearly word for word, with a few deletions and changes for clarity or privacy.

For demographics, Javier is in his mid-fifties, married to a woman, but he has sex almost exclusively with men. That part isn't important. Here's what is:

"Regarding bathhouses, and more specifically, [a certain monthly sex party at a private residence], for me, the thing that I find so fulfilling is less the sex than the ability to re-experience male nudity in a way that is non-threatening. Unlike high school, or health clubs where straight muscle men preen for the seemingly sole purpose of waiting for the gays to finally lose control and take a quick peek, which can then allow them to sneer, at a bathhouse or orgy I can look all I like. I'm not being creepy, and I am not in danger. I can relive a locker room experience as celebratory rather than shaming. For me, there is something so comforting about sitting on [the party host's] sofa with a beer, sandwiched between three other naked men, my left hand in the long hair of the man on my left, my right hand twining through the silky pubic hair of the man on my right while watching a parade of naked men of every shape and shade walk by, and stop and chat, cocks casually in my face to be stared at or not, as I am inclined. For me, it's just so relaxing."

The other two guys (both of whom I'd hooked up with, incidentally) told me the same basic thing. They enjoy this queer male space for what it is: men who are attracted to men, making this completely normal. That is not a luxury we get in the straight world. Queer people are less likely than straight folks to take sex for granted. The novelty of being able to have sex with another man still hasn't quite worn off for me. I still look over my shoulder when I so much as hold hands with a man in public, and I'm thirty-five years old.

The rules *are* different for queer people when it comes to sex and dating. Straight men have brothels; queer men have bathhouses. Queer men don't *need* brothels, though we certainly do have our own sex workers. Nonetheless, gay culture and straight culture are looking more and more alike. While straight people get more used to kink, polyamory, gender play, etc., queers get more and more into traditional relationships.

In the same text chain as above, Javier told me that he's often surprised at how many guys have no qualms asking for their fetishes to be fulfilled, from S&M to being urinated on, but they're shy about asking for attentive, gentle affection. He went on:

"I find it interesting that most sex workers of both persuasions seem to report that the 'boyfriend' or 'girlfriend' experience is what seems to be most requested. Gone are the days (sort of) when you had to pay to be whipped or handcuffed. Now you pay for affection and intimacy."

Intimacy and affection. That's the big thing people are fantasizing about once again. We can see this trend in gay porn as well. About twelve years ago, I noticed that American gay porn was getting a lot more intimate. We could call it "affection porn," the antithesis of "torture porn" in the horror genre. This trend towards connection and intimacy was probably learned from the Czech porn titans Bel Ami Studios, who have traditionally featured affectionate, smiling fellows giving as much as taking pleasure. Following in Bel Ami's steps were American studios like Corbin Fisher, Sean Cody, and the absolutely succulent Cocky Boys. These studios often eschew the plot, which is usually a stupid device in porn. Instead of a hokey plot, there's now a narrative of what these two (or more) men like about one another, perhaps how they met, etc. Cocky Boys in particular is pioneering the new porn narrative, which includes well-lit, well-shot, well-edited interviews with the models as they explain their attraction to one another.

Porn is for fantasy. It seems that the most common fantasy for queer American men is now intimate connection, getting to know someone first, building sexual attraction and tension, and communicating. The marriage-equality movement is closely connected to this. Before Bel Ami's influence, American gay porn was basically a lot of models faking enthusiasm while grunting about sticking it in. I'm no academic porn expert, but I've watched a lot of it since I turned eighteen, and this is what I've seen unfold over the last decade and a half.

Gay culture leans more and more into intimacy, connection, and affection, and that is another promise of PrEP. Whether you pair PrEP with condoms or not, PrEP is shattering one of the biggest psychological blocks to real intimacy. The confidence and ease that PrEP brings me actually leads me to meet more compatible guys for relationships. There was a time that I felt I couldn't date an HIV-positive man. That worry mostly evaporated with the poz-undetectable status, and PrEP took care of any other fear of infection through casual encounters.

I WAS VERY lucky to grow up with little shame in my household; the fact that my parents are former flower children probably has a lot to do with that. I was never taught to be ashamed of being a sexual human. They never told me that being gay was bad. Promiscuity itself was rarely judged, though I was taught that I should care about the people with whom I have sex. I wasn't taught that masturbation was wrong. It was just a thing people do. It wasn't outright encouraged, but it was just a human thing. My mother recently told me that I went through a penis-touching phase when I was about five (I have no memory of masturbating before the age of ten), and she would just turn away and let me do my thing.

When I was about twelve or thirteen, my sister Danielle gave me the masturbation talk one night, much to my surprise. I don't think my parents put her up to it. I'm sure my dad would've figured out how to bring it up if it were an issue. Danielle was already out of the house and on her own; she's ten years older than me. Maybe she was visiting for a holiday or something. She was fixing her hair and makeup in the bathroom. I kept her company. We became closer and closer throughout my teens, especially as my parents had rough times in their marriage. Danielle was always there to rescue me.

Danielle casually rolled a strip of blond hair around her curling iron. "Have you started masturbating yet?"

The honest answer was *Yes, every day! Sometimes two or three times!* but what I said in my gobstopped shock was, "No! No. Uh-uh."

"It's fine if you do. It's normal. Just keep it to yourself." She applied some eyeliner. The dexterity needed to operate a curling iron while applying eye makeup is beyond me. I can't even play drums.

I'm not sure why she brought masturbation up and then suggested I keep it to myself. Had I been talking about it? Maybe I'd been overheard talking to friends. Maybe I'd left evidence. Who knows. I'd probably left a lot of evidence.

But that's about the extent of shame in my house: "Keep it to yourself." I was never given the impression I was a bad person for anything I did. This context is essential for readers to understand my feelings about queer sex and and gender. All of these were considered okay in my family. My parents didn't *want* me to be gay or genderqueer, but they're very supportive. My sister loves it, and she tells me I'm the best parts of having a brother and a sister. She has another brother from her dad (we have different fathers), but she never got to have a sister. She likes to put side-by-side pics of her other brother and me on Facebook, the linebacker mowing the lawn with his shirt off, me luxuriating in a fur coat. Not that I'm against mowing the lawn with my shirt off, mind you. Totes masc, bro.

I'm grateful for my loving, supportive family. I bring this up because I got through life with much less internalized homophobia than a lot of queer people have. That's important for the following conversation. I'm in no way a fluke, but the shame around sex and being queer is a powerful block to things like self care, which includes PrEP and other forms of prevention.

The internalized homophobia is still there, mind you; I question my gender presentation on most days. *Do I look too faggy? Should I act more masculine in a certain situation? Will I be a target for violence? Should I decide to do a butch look for a certain party rather than a femme or genderfuck look?* I pray to Saint David Bowie, and he tells me to be strong and do it 100%, no half-steppin'.

There is still a huge amount of shame among queer people. It's picked up everywhere, from the family home to the church to the social climate of school and the street. I learned most of my self-doubt and homophobia at school, since we had gays in the family and my folks never once took me to a church or synagogue.

When it came to sex, I'm not sure if I had "shame" so much as I had a mix of frustration, regret, and longing. When I first started hooking up at age eighteen, I often felt empty afterwards, and the sex itself was often boring and awkward.

I tried my best in college and my twenties to be promiscuous, but I really just wanted to be loved by the person with whom I was getting naked and slippery. I tried having a couple of three-ways, but those were terribly disappointing. Perhaps it was the company. My advice: if you're going to have a three-way, make sure you're attracted to both the people. If you're unfortunate, the one you don't like is going to want to do all the things to you, while the one you're hot for will mostly observe.

I continued looking for love in all the wrong places, but that's because I was codependent, not because I'm gay. I must've turned down plenty of stellar guys because I couldn't deal with what they brought to the table, even when it was exactly what I needed. Even so, when I was having disappointing (or worse) sex with people who didn't give a crap about me, I wasn't ashamed of myself.

Frustrated, disappointed, even desperate, sure. But I was not ashamed.

Just to clarify, most psychological sources that I've read break down the difference between guilt and shame in this way: guilt is about something you did. Shame is about something you *are*.

I encounter plenty of guys online and in person who have no qualms about PrEP, but I've also meet a lot of guys who refuse to take it. This is a separate group from the guys who come across as calm and confident that PrEP isn't right for them after giving it some practical thought. That group is growing, or so I've observed. However, the men who absolutely refuse to take PrEP are a separate cohort.

Of these guys, about a third tell me that they're against taking pharmaceuticals in general. They don't trust Big Pharma, or they're into naturopathic alternatives, or they just don't like taking any drug they don't absolutely need. I sympathize with this group. I went through the same qualms in deciding whether to get on PrEP.

The other two-thirds of the PrEP dissidents have offered many different excuses:

"I don't participate in risky behavior very often."

"PrEP is for guys who just want to bareback and have lots of partners."

"I'm afraid of how it might change my behavior."

"No one needs PrEP! Why don't people just use a condom every time?"

Behind every one of these statements is the same basic sentiment: *I don't want to feel ashamed of myself or my actions.* Put another way: *I'm afraid PrEP will make me a dirty slut, and then I'll judge myself.*

Heaven help us. I hear all sorts of dressed-up excuses, and again and again they all come back to the same thing. People are afraid that PrEP will somehow convince them they're invincible, and that being invincible means they'll end up in the park late at night with their pants down, touching their toes, with a sign taped to their ass that says "Please fuck me like the nasty little piggy that I am." Not that they'd ever do that without PrEP. Surely not.

The real underlying fear here isn't that they'll become promiscuous. The actual fear is of the shame they'll experience if they become promiscuous.

HIV has only made the shame situation worse. Gay people don't merely deal with shame over being attracted to the same sex. Gay men are not just ashamed of actually having sex with another man. We also get ashamed that we did something risky to our health. Thanks a lot, AIDS crisis.

The shame is compounded—the desire, the activity, and the perceived lack of health precaution, all layering to become a McShamewich of neuroses. Plus that extra layer about not being masculine enough. You wonder why gay guys can be so neurotic? It's because for over thirty years we were told that our sexual orientation is so effectively destructive that it will not only send us to Hell, it'll be the very thing that kills us.

See another example: on the apps, particularly on Scruff, a lot of guys use the term "clean" when they mean they've tested negative for all STIs. "Clean"—the opposite of dirty, marked, or unsanitary. The implications are clear.

The backlash against the term "clean" has also been palpable. There was a meme for a while of guys taking their profile pic in the shower, a social campaign to recognize that "clean" doesn't mean "disease free" just as "dirty" doesn't mean "diseased." It sure is easy to judge sexual behavior when there's a deadly disease being spread by sex—except that HIV isn't deadly anymore if you have access to proper care.

That's actually part of the threat that PrEP represents: people are so attached to their shame around unprotected or promiscuous sex, and PrEP means they'll have to find a new excuse to judge themselves and others for any mildly risky behavior.

Oops! I gave you head on the first date, and I accidentally bit my lip this morning—I hope you don't give me AIDS. Now I hate myself. Don't look at me ever again. Get out.

I know that I cling to the things that scare me and hurt me sometimes; clinging to them is familiar. It's easier to sit idle and be afraid that I'll never make it as an author, rather than to actually write a book. It's easier to be afraid of HIV than to learn how it actually works, how to prevent it, and all the many options available. I see other gay men clinging to the fear of HIV and shame around sex, and rejecting PrEP is a way of holding onto those fears and shames rather than resolving them.

Taking Truvada is the exact opposite of sexual recklessness. Taking Truvada daily is precisely an act of sexual responsibility, whether you combine it with condoms or not.

This self-shaming is literally killing us. It always has been. Shame causes us to hide things and to hide *from* things. Shame causes us to resent ourselves, and this gets worse. Shame leads us to hate and hurt ourselves rather than to know our value and refuse to hurt ourselves.

Shame does not work as a deterrent. When I went through twelve-step recovery for codependency, I learned just how ineffective shame is in changing anyone's behavior. Listening to the stories of many addicts, sex addicts in particular but many others as well, taught me this about shame: it makes us feel worthless. Worthlessness makes us keep hurting ourselves and others, because we don't feel like it's worth it to change. When we shame someone for their feelings and desires, to say nothing of their actions, we teach them not to stop desiring and acting but to start hiding. This is why I'm against social justice advocates shaming people for saying or doing the wrong thing; shame doesn't make people clean up their act, if there's even something to clean up. Plus shame is a tool of homophobia and misogyny, so why use it to end prejudice?

Most addicts become excellent at hiding the evidence of their behavior because of shame. If there were no shame, why would anyone hide anything? For a surprise birthday party? If we can see how shame works in addictive patterns, we can see how it works in the healthy and powerful instinct to have sex.

When you're the one calling yourself shameful, it becomes even more insidious. In the case of all the people I've heard objecting to PrEP when they themselves could use it, this shame isn't stopping the sex. Instead, it's stopping people from talking to their doctors about getting a prescription for Truvada. It's stopping people from showing up to clinics to get tested. This has always been one of the biggest challenges to HIV prevention: how to make people feel safe enough to go get tested. People avoid HIV tests because they don't want to face the results. People also avoid getting tested because they don't want anyone to know their sexual practices.

Shame, shame, shame. Here's to thousands of years of ineffective shame, to lives and reputations ruined, to families broken, to incarceration for victimless crimes, all because someone thought someone else is shameful.

Screw that. I'll just take my Truvada and my chances. I have very little to hide. I'm with the guys on social media who use the tag #TruvadaWhore to reclaim that term and show that actually, we're quite responsible about our sexual health.

Ten

#TruvadaWhore

30 tablets

℞ only

I HATCHED A plan to seduce Scott.

I had met him during my fourth-step work in recovery, while I was avoiding Kent and sex and dating in general. Everett, our mutual mentor, introduced us and encouraged us to go out for coffee together. When Everett matches me with someone, I take that very seriously.

My fourth step only lasted about six weeks. Scott could wait. If he couldn't wait, he wasn't a good match.

He waited. We tried going on dates. That didn't last long. Then he had a shamanic soul retrieval and whatever soul parts he got back needed him to go out and sow his sexy oats, and I was not into that idea. After the dark night of the soul that was step four, I was in a boyfriendy mood, not a fuckfriendy mood.

Flashing forward a year, things were different. I knew Scott was on PrEP, and around the time I began taking Truvada, I had a dream about him:

We were in a classroom, and I was a student. Scott was teaching. I think I knew some of the other students, but I can't remember who most of them were. Scott told me that I needed to take my medicine, but I refused. He had a tablespoon full of chalky pink liquid, like Pepto Bismol, and I shut my mouth tight, teeth gritted together.

The other students held me down and pulled down my pants. Scott poured the dose of medicine into the crack of my ass, essentially administering it anally. The dream ended.

I figured this dream was sexual. I mean, *duh*. But it was also about my fears of getting onto PrEP. All my fears of taking a medicine that I didn't technically need—like the antispasmodics or antidepressants prescribed to me by Dr. S, that crankbird. There was the fear that it might wreak havoc on my digestive system, the integrity of which I take very seriously. There were my aunt's staunch warnings about taking any HIV medicine, especially when I didn't even carry the virus. There was probably some resentment towards Scott in there as well.

I decided to text him and tell him all about the dream. Since we're both woo-woo witchy magic Pagan homos, a little dream interpretation would be a great way to bring up the topic of us finally doing the deed. It even felt like foreplay, albeit a bit absurd.

Scott: *You said the liquid was chalky and thick?*

EJP: *Yeah. Pink and chalky.*

Scott: *Like semen.*

EJP: *Yes, dorkface, like semen. Except pink.*

Scott: *Hmmm. And I literally put it in your butt?*

EJP: *Well, kinda, you poured it into my crack.*

Scott: *How did that feel, in the dream?*

EJP: *What, like emotionally or physically? Physically, it felt cold and slimy. Emotionally, it felt embarrassing and angering, like you were dominating me or bullying me.*

Scott:	*Do you want someone to dominate and humiliate you?*
EJP:	*Not particularly, no. Not my fetish.*
Scott:	*Maybe you actually do.*
EJP:	*Drop it, Scott. I'm not ready for that.*
Scott:	*Okay, sorry. Is this your first sex dream about me?*
EJP:	*I think so. But I've been attracted to you for a long time. I mean, you knew that.*

We decided to explore together. Scott had been on PrEP for less than a year, but long enough for his behaviors to shift. His previous off-again-on-again boyfriend is HIV-positive, and PrEP was a great option for him. When that relationship ended, but like for real this time they really mean it, I took the opportunity.

I asked Scott to have sex with me for two reasons: for one, I'd always wanted to go to bed with Scott, and I was finally ready to ask for it. Secondly, I wanted the opportunity to try barebacking, something I'd never allowed myself in all my fourteen years of being sexually active. Come to think of it, the sex with Scott was happening at almost the same time of year as my very first hookup with Justin at eighteen. Hopefully, it would go better. I felt very confident about this—so confident that I want to tell you about it in present tense.

I AM ON the bed. Brunch sits heavily in my stomach, but not so heavily that I'm distracted from what's happening. We went out for French toast with berry compote, a nice little friend date to set the mood.

I am lying on my right side, back to the nightstand with its octopus-shaped lamp and its cubby of medicine bottles, books, and lubes.

Scott is facing me. We're both in underwear. His are nondescript black, clinging briefs. Mine are bright blue. Fun underwear was the first purchase I made when I got a real job after grad school. I'm glad we're already down to our underwear. Scott's jeans were ridiculous, covered in rips that someone planned very strategically. He looks much better out of them.

He's leading. We've been talking about this for weeks. Scott and I kiss on my bed in our underwear. It's about noon, the sunlight filtering from the tiny window that meets the ceiling above my altar corner. The bedroom is almost entirely underground, while the rest of the apartment is diagonally half-in, half-out of the hill. There's a glass prism hanging in the window, a gift from my parents. The sunlight hits it, spraying little rainbows around the room. Today calls for rainbows. Today, I will have condomless sex for the first time in my life. I am thirty-two years old.

Scott has the tiniest gauges I've ever seen in his earlobes. They're bright blue, like my briefs. Between kissing, I tend to stare at his ear jewelry or at his stomach and chest. I don't know why I'm so shy today. He's my friend. We've both wanted this for some time. He smells a little like pine and vetiver.

Underwear comes off. Scott is so sweet with me. He knows this is a big deal for me. He knows that I've never had sex without a condom. He knows I don't even fuck most of the time, unless I'm dating someone. He gets that this is a rite of passage, something bound up in rituals of initiation and manhood. As a shamanic practitioner, Scott's very into such things.

He makes me the center of attention. He warms up my body, gets me relaxed and rock-hard. He gives me some of the best head I've ever had. Then we switch around. He lies down on his back, and I get between his legs. I put a pillow under his tailbone to raise the angle of his ass. I can't remember the last time I topped someone in any way other than face-to-face.

I lube him up. I lube myself up.

"Should we set an intention?" When sex is a rite of initiation, you might as well pray. Gods like when you dedicate a loving fuck to them, and I do love Scott. He loves me too. He's my friend. We ask Spirit to witness us.

I work my way inside him. He's tight, and I try to go slowly. I'm so eager for this, and he asks me to ease up. I do.

I slip in until I can't get in any farther. His body grips onto me, and he's so tight that it's uncomfortable at first. I watch his face as I ease in and out of him. I love the way he looks at me when I'm inside of him—so admirable, so vulnerable, vulnerable because he chooses to be, because he's let me in and wants me to become a part of his own body for as long as that lasts, and I'm giving him kindness and joy and pleasure from the inside outward, and I am the Wand, the God of the Woods, and he is the Cup, the God of the Waters, and I am filling him up with the sky, and we are doing what all gods want their children to do. We are loving each other with our bodies as well as our hearts.

I CAN'T RECALL if I came inside him or not. I don't think that was the point.

I'm not sure if sex was more intimate without a condom. The sex was intimate because it was with Scott.

There is one more truth to tell about this experience, a truth that I think is extraordinarily important: topping Scott without a condom didn't feel significantly better—physically—than past experiences with condoms. It was different, but it wasn't as though Cupid tied a star to my cock. The difference was mainly emotional.

I step back from this experience wondering whether the resistance to condoms is more psychological or physical. The bottoms I've interviewed have frequently said that they hate condoms, and that latex irritates them quickly, while bare skin allows them to get fucked for much longer. As a top, however, I found the difference slim between wearing one and not wearing one.

I've found the right condoms for my body—Trojan Ecstasy, which have more room at the top of the penis, where I have most of my sensitivity. Put a little lube in there and it makes things much better. Then again, as Javier told me, "I too discovered that lube inside a Trojan Ecstasy was almost indistinguishable from bareback topping. The problem? Of the twelve I bought, four of them broke. Yet another reason to go for Truvada."

I've also found better lube—silicone based, which has a nice friction and drag to it and doesn't dry up as quickly as ultra-slippery water-based lube. Silicone feels so much better than the watery gloop. Thanks to great friends like Angelo Bomasuto, an HIV counselor in Florida, who got me into silicone lube and taught me to put a little inside the condom first in order to get more stimulation.

Or maybe it's because I've only had sex without a condom once. It seems like I have a pattern of not liking something sexual the first time I do it, then loving it later. My love life has been as random as ever in the two years since I had sex with Scott, and I haven't been with any one person long enough to feel right about it. James was a fluke, dancing just out of reach. Jake peaced-out on me after the fourth date, even though he'd said he wanted to date seriously. Shaun and I broke up after four months for several reasons, one of which was sexual incompatibility. Apollo and I just never went there, but we had a great time doing everything else.

THAT BRINGS ME to James. I began dating James right after getting on PrEP, and right after I'd had my encounter with Scott. Okay, okay—James and I had gone on two dates already when I fucked Scott. But James likes to take things remarkably slowly, so we hadn't even kissed yet. Don't hate the player; hate the game.

James was also in the process of getting onto PrEP, although I never figured out why. He was one of the most sexually restrained people I've ever dated. He's not asexual, but he made it clear while we were dating that he wanted to wait until he felt right about it before having sex. This went on for three months, up to and including dates several nights a week, sleeping over, cuddling and making out in our underwear, and some other above the waist shenanigans.

I was crazy about him, yet another pattern: infatuated by people who are unavailable in some way or another. I'd had a crush on James for years; he worked at my neighborhood branch of the library. I wanted to spend a coma asleep on his chest. For this reason, I almost stopped taking PrEP within three months of getting onto the drug.

I liked James so much that I was completely willing to wait, and wait some more, before we had any form of sex. We didn't even jerk off together. This was an experiment for me. It had been years since I truly devoted myself to getting to know someone before we did anything below the belt. I also stopped dating and hooking up with other people while I was seeing him. I felt like a Mormon, but also nothing like one.

What irony—I was in the process of writing a definitive personal essay on what it means to be on PrEP and all the conversations people were having about it, and I found myself magically in a functionally exclusive, temporarily celibate relationship with a great guy who happened to be HIV-negative. At a certain point during this period of abstinence before consummation, I contacted my HIV specialist, Dr. Kathy Brown, and told her I was thinking about going off PrEP.

Here's our email exchange:

"Hi, Dr. Kathy! Great news. I have had no physical side effects on PrEP so far. *The Stranger* article comes out next month!

I'm also dating someone HIV-negative and also on PrEP (and he's amazing and adorable). It's not serious yet, but it looks like it could easily get monogamous in the near future. I don't know what that means for my future taking PrEP, but I anticipate that I may stop taking it if indeed we become monogamous. Any thoughts/feedback on that?"

"Hi Evan! I've been looking for your article, glad to hear it is coming out soon!

If you are both truly monogamous then neither of you need to be on PrEP. You can stop it and restart it if you need it again at some point. Each time you restart it you have to wait 1-2 weeks before it reaches a protective level in the blood and rectal tissue.

Sounds like you think he's pretty special!"

I did think James was pretty special. Like, *stop seeing other people and wait months before having sex* kind of special. I don't require lots of sex. I tend to have frequent new partners, but I can go months without it. What I require is that anyone I date is affectionate and wants to spend time with me.

We went to fancy restaurants, we went to see plays, we cooked together, and we made out constantly. My heart almost exploded the first time I kissed him.

Toward the third month, James began to withdraw very slowly. He was clearly depressed and irritable. He was applying to grad schools across the country, another reason he was being so slow with me—in case he had a golden opportunity to move away. I thought good and long about moving with him or asking for long distance, which I swore in the oughts that I would never, ever,

ever do again.

I gave James time. I gave him space. I was tempted to have sex with others, but I never did. I had something to prove to myself. I kept taking my PrEP.

I told him the night before Thanksgiving that he was still worth waiting for. We hadn't seen one another in several weeks, and he invited me over to keep him company while he baked artisanal pies. Damn your artisanal baking, James. Damn your bourbon-and-bacon-infused apple pies.

We had a good talk, but after not seeing him in weeks, I thought he looked like shit, and not a big-eyed smiling poop emoji. My beautiful guy, with his large hazel eyes and his peaceful smile, was instead squinting, pinched, his usually neat black hair uncombed, his chin unshaven for days when I had been used to seeing his face smooth as a crystal ball.

While the pies were in the oven, I perched on a stool in his kitchen and picked up little scraps of garlic paper from around the counter and put them in the trash.

"I miss you, James. A lot. Do you think you'll feel better soon, and we'll go back to the way things were?"

He took his glasses off but didn't look at me. "Quite possibly."

In retrospect, I see what a lousy-ass jerk he was to me, and what a lousy-ass jerk I was for sticking around for so long. But when I was in the middle of dating my longtime crush, I thought I was the luckiest recovering-codependent kid on the block.

"I miss holding you, James. Kissing you. Hearing you talk about your life. You haven't been available for that lately. Do you think you'll be available again soon? Maybe in January, when all your applications are in?"

He was very quiet. James is almost always very quiet.

He stared down and said, "I think so."

That was good enough for the moment. As the pies baked, we watched a couple of episodes of *Archer* in separate armchairs. I wanted to cuddle but was afraid to ask him to. I really wanted to put his whole face in my mouth and swish it around in there for days.

When I left, he held me close and kissed me. He said, "I'm sorry I'm like this right now. Thank you for putting up with me."

I leaned my forehead against his and said, "You're still worth waiting for."

This was the last time I saw him. I got sick of him taking more than a day to return my texts, and then all he'd write was, *Hey! I don't know when I'll be able to hang out this week. Sorry.* Maybe he was avoiding me. Maybe he wanted me to initiate the breakup. That stopped being worth waiting for.

I left him a voice mail after the first week of December. I'd rather have said it in person, but he wasn't available and this needed to get done. I thought about Thomas expecting me to drive five hours to see him, just so we wouldn't break up over the phone.

"Hi, James. Ummmm—I want you to know that I accept that this isn't working out between us. I've had a wonderful time getting to know you these past few months. Annnnd—I love you. Soooo—goodbye."

He never responded. He didn't even respond when I texted him to wish him a Merry Christmas a few weeks later. I'd never told him I loved him before then, but I knew I did. It seemed the best way to break up with him.

I stayed on PrEP.

I went home to see my folks in Florida for the holidays. I didn't go fuck my heartache away, which is what I'd usually attempt half-heartedly after a break up, especially with an aloof dreamboat like James.

But then it was January. Time to get down to business.

I WENT LATE to get tickets for a play at the University of Washington with my friend Swope. Swope is a brilliant digital artist who moonlights as the drag queen Heavy Scene Macaque.

Swope and I waited around for the ticket holders to take their seats for a production of *The Picture of Dorian Gray*. I love that story. I named my dog after that story. We ducked into a side room of the theater building, wherein the theater students swanned about and played board games and discussed the nuances of *RuPaul's Drag Race* and the Theatre of Cruelty. In Seattle, theater majors come and go, talking of Antonin Artaud.

A big-eyed, bristly little dude slumped on one couch. He and I eye-fucked each other for several minutes, but I didn't make a move. I'd seen him often on

Scruff. Twenty-one years old, younger than the usual Scruff crowd, but good on him for knowing who and what he wanted. I hadn't ever contacted him, perhaps had never read his profile, because his pic didn't do much for me.

This is a big lesson I've learned from the dating apps and sites: A person's pictures lie. I don't mean they lie like Markus lied when he featured a suave, decade-old pic of himself captaining a sailboat and then showed up to our date looking like a wad of chewed gum. I mean that pictures capture only a nanosecond in time. Those of us lucky enough to understand the power of body language, lighting, and facial expression can create pics of ourselves that reflect not only our personalities but also our raw sex appeal, all in a fraction of a moment. Knowing how the hell photography works helps. But hey, when you have abs and good hair, you can just take a pic of yourself in a dirty mirror, flyblown with scum from your flicked dental floss and pinched zits, and everyone will want to fuck you, but two-thirds of us will be too intimidated by your awesome body to actually talk to you. Here's looking at you, Seattle.

The lesson: clean your goddamn mirror before you take a selfie.

Actually, no, that's a side point. The lesson here is that it's uncommon for someone's pics to show what they truly look like. What you look like isn't just your nose, your chest, your dingaling. It's the way you arch your brows when you're impressed. It's your posture, the way you smirk when I tell you I want to do terribly wonderful things to you in my bedroom. Until someone meets you in person and smells your pheromones and watches the way you lick your lips when you're deep in thought, people won't know how sexy you truly are. Most of us are better looking in person than in our pics, myself included, yet I'm just as guilty as anyone else of seeing profile pics and saying, "Meh."

I did that with Arnold, the bristly theater student on the couch. But after seeing him in person and recognizing him, I thought, *Why not? Why am I being so aloof about this stuff?* True, he was only twenty-one, much younger than my established cut-off age for serious dating. But I didn't need anything serious to occupy me after James. No, a slightly awkward twink who was dying to jump on my D was just what the doctor ordered.

Swope and I did not get to the theater in time to gain late tickets to the show. Instead, we went back to his place and got baked, ate cookies, and played one of our favorite games: *Judging People on Grindr.* Sometimes we judge so hard that I break a sweat and have to take a break from all the judging. In our defense, we don't make fun of people for their weight or other easy targets for bullying. We make fun of people for their egregious lack of taste:

"Fuck's sake, what is this one wearing? Who pairs a see-through golfing visor with a thong?"

"Can it still be called a thong if he doesn't have an ass? I'd call that a slingshot."

"Two snaps for Miss Dennis the Menace over here."

"It's like his back just keeps going down to his feet. I bet his asshole looks like a bellybutton."

"Oooh, speaking of feet. This profile says he wants someone to get drunk or stoned and pass out while he does fetishy stuff with their feet."

"Right. I'm going to go to your house and let you literally drug me so you can molest me while I'm passed out. Is he, like, straight or something?"

I signed into Scruff instead. "Hey! There's that guy I was eye-flirting with at the theater building. Do you know him?"

I showed him Arnold's profile.

"Nope, don't recognize him."

By this point, I had decided to play my micro-celebrity card and simultaneously spread the word about PrEP by talking about the *Stranger* article in my Scruff profile. Just a little tag to say, "Google this if you want to find out more about me."

I told Swope, "I'm going to woof at him and see what happens."

Well. Here's what happened.

EJP:	*Weren't we giving each other the eye over at the theater building?*
Arnold:	*Yep. Thanks for woofing. So you're the guy who wrote the PrEP article?*
EJP:	*I did! I like to brag about it a little.*
Arnold:	*It was great. It helped me finally make a decision to get on PrEP.*

EJP:	*I'm so glad I could help! Yeah, it's shocking that so many people haven't heard about it.*
Arnold:	*I had heard about it, just wasn't sure if it was for me. But I've been on it for a month now.*
EJP:	*Yeah? So you should be good to go on protection. Have you had a chance to hook up while on it?*
Arnold:	*Not yet. Maybe you could help with that.*
EJP:	*Would love to. What do you like to do?*
Arnold:	*I'm a bottom.*
EJP:	*Yeah, I noticed. We can do that if it feels right. But besides that, what turns you on?*
Arnold:	*Well, I like to…*

Readers can use their imaginations at this point. Some mystery is good for the libido.

The conversation got so hot that we decided to jerk off together while we sexted. Did I mention I love sexting? We traded descriptions of some of our favorite things, and it only made us hotter for one another leading up to meeting in person.

We hooked up three times, and two of those were explosive. We tried some improv games. We're both performers, after all. The first time we had sex, at one point I told him to pretend that I'm a straight guy in his class that he's been hot for all quarter, and now I've suddenly decided to try hooking up with him. *Give it to me like that.* The result was some of the best first-time sex I've ever had with a new partner. Sex was definitely getting better on PrEP.

IT WAS 2015. PrEP was in wide use, and yet I still met people frequently who had no idea of its existence. I wrote an article about it for TheBody.com[5] and continued to write about it in *The Stranger*. Here are some highlights of what I learned.

Damon L. Jacobs asked, "How could we have a medical tool to end HIV transmissions, have support of legislators around the U.S., insurance coverage, support from the CDC, WHO, and HRC, front page coverage on the New York Times (5/15/14) and still people don't know about it?"

Damon is a New York City psychotherapist and PrEP educator. He's also administrator of the Facebook group "PrEP Facts: Rethinking HIV Prevention and Sex."

Most times when I go for my mandatory quarterly PrEP blood tests, as I'm waiting for the needle to slip into my vein, I make nervous small talk with the phlebotomist. The tech usually isn't familiar with the term "PrEP." Even the lesbians who've drawn my blood have outed themselves as not being very familiar with it. There are reasons for that—it's not every lab tech's job to be familiar with prescription medications. But the pharmacy tech? And the actual nurses? Nurses still get emphatic training on how to avoid transmission of HIV during needle procedures. Why aren't there units in their training about PrEP?

When I called my insurance provider's consulting nurse service about flu-like symptoms, the nurse encouraged me not to rule out seroconversion (i.e., becoming HIV-positive), even though I assured her that I had taken Truvada religiously for six months, had not had sex in more than a month, and tested negative for HIV two weeks prior. A nurse has to be cautious, of course, but I got the impression that she really didn't understand the nature of PrEP. She kept bringing up seroconversion as a possibility, even though the possibility was zero. What does that really tell us about the state of the current medical field, even in a highly liberal and heavily queer-populated city like my current home of Seattle?

I eventually found out that my chart lists "exposure to HIV," leading one friend to joke that I have the word S-L-U-T written in red across my file. Other nurses were similarly confused, thinking I was on PEP, post-exposure treatment, a common regimen for medical workers who've had an accidental blood exposure on the job. The simple, direct, but open-ended tag of "exposure to HIV" could mean damn near anything, but in my case it means that I occasionally have sex with HIV-positive people, all of whom so far have told me they're undetectable (which is the norm, not the exception).

Weekly, sometimes daily, I encounter people who have no clue what PrEP is. More people don't know what it is when I bring it up. It remains occult knowledge known only to a certain sub-demographic of queer people. Straight people, lesbians, and queer men who live outside LGBTQ subculture are all about as likely to ask me, "What's PrEP?" as they are to ask me, "What's an 'otter'?" or "Who the hell is Venus Xtravaganza?"

Do we really live in a culture in which the daily prevention pill for HIV—a disease which has been considered a global pandemic, a disease which has afflicted seventy-eight million human beings of all ages, races, sexualities, and genders—is just kind of not a big deal?

In one word: yes. We live at a time in which the most effective measure ever invented for preventing HIV has flown under the radar, at least of the general American public, and it's being ignored by many even in the gay community.

Damon told me he believes it's a combination of homophobia, sex-negativity, politics, and "the simple human reluctance to change."

"I think there is a level of willful denial that gay people are having sex, much less anal sex. You can let them get married, but you can't let them enjoy sex with one or more partners." But Damon doesn't simply throw the straight community under the bus—he's equally critical of the gay ignorance of what PrEP is and what it does.

"There is a complacent denial amongst gay/bisexual men who don't know about PrEP. They may spend time focusing on advances in marital equality, but are shut down to progress in sexual pleasure and freedom. They may be up-to-date on issues affecting Obamacare, but couldn't care less about preventing HIV."

Please note that he told this to me in early 2015, and things have changed since then, but they haven't changed that much. Damon lives in New York City, which is one of the AIDS capitals of America. How can queers in New York City not know about PrEP? It's beyond an income thing. Even if a New Yorker is too poor to afford internet access and other access to information, there are posters up around the city.

My friend Chris Nelson, a gay man and registered nurse who now attends Johns Hopkins, first heard about PrEP from some of the Sisters of Perpetual Indulgence, a movement of drag queen nuns who preach sexual health and queer pride.

Although PrEP is a relatively recent development in HIV prevention, it indicates much that Nelson heard about it from his gay peers before his professional colleagues at the hospital. He vacillated on whether or not to get on the medication, due in no small part to the amount of contradictory information floating around and the fiery debates about the drug's effectiveness.

Chris eventually made up his mind. "I started PrEP on January 1, 2015 as a New Year's resolution: I will protect my health."

Other friends, particularly straight friends, had never heard of PrEP until they heard about it from me. Heather Snookal, a Seattle-area science teacher, was surprised and concerned that she'd never heard of a breakthrough like PrEP until late 2014. She has since begun integrating PrEP awareness into her curriculum.

Mariah Crystal Ortiz, another straight friend, had just returned to the United States after working with the Peace Corps in Namibia. Despite working directly with HIV-positive people who were receiving anti-retroviral (ARV) treatment, Ortiz hadn't heard of PrEP until November 2014, after reading my original *Stranger* article after returning to the U.S. She also mentioned that while she believes that "free ARVs help uphold the basic human right to health," she found that "there is some debate in Namibia about whether providing free ARVs promotes careless behavior." This sounds awfully similar to the sex-shaming around PrEP that we hear constantly.

I again queried my friends David Kern and Richard Aleshire from the Washington Health Department (David has since become Deputy Commissioner of the HIV/STI bureau at the Chicago Department of Public Health). They frequently collaborated on the emails they sent me. "We think [the continued lack of public knowledge is] a function of the newness of PrEP. We don't imagine most communities have followed PrEP developments over the years… Since PrEP hit the mainstream media [in 2014], we've seen a measurable increase in awareness, and we anticipate interest will continue to increase." Remember that this information is two years old as of this book's printing, but that doesn't make it very far from our current state of understanding.

There was more to it as well, overlapping with what Damon told me. "It may have something to do with 'AIDS-fatigue' in general," Kern and Aleshire asserted. "People do not show as much interest in anything related to HIV/AIDS as they used to."

Lest we forget, PrEP doesn't exist in a vacuum. From a public health standpoint, it's a new development in the overall fight against HIV infections. Kern and Aleshire also told me, "We need to move outside of our separate 'prevention' and 'care' boxes and see the whole continuum, the whole person, and provide services both to people not yet infected and those who are, without having to rely on the specific stream of funding."

Ultimately, the answer to the question of why more people don't know that PrEP exists isn't completely cut-and-dried. No question that huge usually is. However, this big issue leads us to the even bigger issue: people have found more enticing issues to care about than ending the HIV/AIDS crisis. Zika is in this season. Breast cancer: still in. Autism and the anti-vaccine movement are on the way out. AIDS is way out of vogue, and HIV-positive people are often pissed about that.

THAT BRINGS ME back to my friend Ian, the one who introduced me to Kent. Kent and I went out to Diesel, a favorite watering hole for the gay bear community, and met up with Ian one night shortly after the *Stranger* article came out. I was gloating.

"People were tweeting about my article in Spanish! I'm famous! Sort of." I sipped my gin and tonic and peacocked around. The bears did not fall into line to kiss my hand.

"Ugh," Ian grunted.

"What, Ian?" From my peripheral vision, I noticed Kent taking a step backward and turning to talk to Javier.

Ian got into it. "PrEP is changing the whole HIV conversation. It's making

HIV-negative people the loudest voices in the HIV conversation, when it's the people living with HIV who should have the biggest platform."

I chewed on that for a few days. In fact, two years later, I'm still chewing on it. Ian is one of the feistiest, most outspoken people I know, and even when they're criticizing me, I'm reminded that they have a brilliant mind and we're usually on the same side of the bigger fight for freedom and justice. I made up my mind to interview Ian. Here's what they told me:

"I attribute lack of knowledge around PrEP almost entirely to a general disinterest on HIV issues. Since the advent of HAART ["highly active antiretroviral therapy"], with the increasing quality of life for those living with HIV who have access to it, a sense of urgency in discussions around HIV has certainly been lacking. People don't view it as deadly anymore and so talk about it less.

"PrEP's impact has been both beneficial and, in some ways, marginalizing to people living with HIV. Happily, it means people are less worried about contracting the virus, so I would say many of us [HIV-positive people] encounter less stigma, though that may not be a majority experience.

"However, the advent of PrEP has meant that a lot of the discussion about HIV is not about HIV-positive people accessing care or about the various other problems someone with HIV faces. Instead we seem to have the advent not just of PrEP, but the 'PrEP warrior.' [HIV-negative] folks are talking about their relation to HIV in a way that means that now instead of [HIV-positive] people being central to the discussion of how best to deal with HIV, neg people are centralizing the discourse around their own experiences. While this is advantageous to those who have yet to contract the virus, it makes me wonder what [HIV-positive] voices—already marginalized—are not being heard."

That's a perspective that needed to be included in this book. I can keep repeating that PrEP is valuable to HIV-positive people for its ways of decreasing stigmas against them, but I am not HIV-positive. This book isn't just about the ways I stay HIV-negative. It's also about eliminating the fear against people who live with HIV. HIV-positive people were silenced in the '80s and left to die. We see how poorly that turned out for everyone.

And now, at long last, the elephant in the room: when is the next STI plague coming? Before HIV, there was syphilis. Syphilis was once a deadly and torturous disease. It rots the mind as well as the body. Now, syphilis is considered as small a threat as measles: it's preventable, it's detectable (though sometimes tricky), and it's treatable. HIV itself has become akin to diabetes, chronic but manageable, without an expected early mortality.

But what's next? There will always be a new disease to deal with, and sometimes these are sexually transmitted. Safer sex isn't just about condoms, and it isn't just about talking to your partner about testing and STI status. Safer sex is about making informed decisions with a clear mind and a sense of self-value. Condoms and PrEP are just two of several tools and options used by people who are being clear-headed and self-valuing. While I encourage everyone to go out and have a good time, and I'm no stranger to sex with, well, *strangers*, I do believe there's a certain mindset of folks who genuinely don't care what happens to their bodies and health, and they act accordingly. Even when I'm picking up a hookup on Scruff, I still care what happens to my body. HIV is something I never worry about contracting. I've also learned that herpes is very common and a lot less trouble than we've been led to believe. I'm still on a fear trip about HPV ("genital" warts). Decades of sex fear take some time to undo, but I'm getting informed about HPV, too.

The stranglehold that HIV gained among men who have sex with men was very much due to the way we were having sex in the late '70s and early '80s. I've made it clear that I do not believe in shaming anyone about sex, but shame should not be confused with forethought and caution. I believe, as do many others, that we can't go back to the way things were before AIDS. If we have unprotected sex with a constant river of anonymous partners, we're going to get some diseases. There will eventually be something new to deal with. I know guys who contract roughly two new STIs per year—syphilis, chlamydia, etc. That seems unnecessary to me.

I almost never contract an STI (knock wood and praise Venus), despite easily having ten new partners in a year or one or two new partners each week when I'm really on fire. Why don't I get more STIs?

There are several reasons. Firstly, I ask my partners if they have an STI and how recently they were tested. In fact, now that I'm on PrEP, I have the confidence boost of starting that conversation by saying, "Hey, so I'm on PrEP, and I don't care one way or another about your HIV status, as long as you know it. Do you know your HIV status? Uh-huh, what about other STIs? Uh-huh, how recently were you tested?" To reiterate my friend Gwen, these conversations aren't sexy. I lose some potential opportunities to hook up when I have these conversations, but that's okay. As Everett once almost yelled at me during a session, "If you tell someone what you really want and your boundaries and they run away, GOOD!"

Sometimes guys tell me that they have an STI, or they recently had one. I make decisions about what to do with them sexually from there. I hope I never again fall for the line I heard in Tallahassee one night—"Oh, these little patches of crusty, honey-colored rash? I had a staph infection. But the doctor says I'm not contagious." Either that doctor was an idiot or my little friend was lying. I caught that staph infection early, and it was still difficult to treat.

Secondly, in order to have these conversations, I meet sexual partners one by one, and I take a little time to talk before leaving a bar with them, inviting them over via phone app, etc. Part of this is my own set of sexual turn-ons; I feel less aroused with an anonymous stranger than I do once I've talked to someone for a bit and gotten a sense of who he is and isn't. The small talk gets me hotter, or maybe it just relieves me enough to let my guard down. The small talk also tends to indicate who's going to be a good time and who is going to be pushy, abusive, untrustworthy, or so nervous that he can't enjoy himself. I used to be that guy who was too nervous to really have a good time. I can relate.

Some people get a big thrill from anonymous sex, sex without names or even words exchanged. If that's your thrill, do what you like, and be cautious. I try to meet people in person in a neutral place before we go back to someone's house, but I'd be telling you a bald-faced lie if I said this is what I do every time. I do it roughly 50-70% of the time.

Third, I still use condoms for anal sex. While PrEP has brought me a fearlessness around HIV, it's made it necessary for me to be more mindful about genital warts, etc. I'm also not alone in having anal sex much less often than oral. I hear frequently from the guys with whom I hook up that butt sex isn't something they usually do outside of a relationship. I'm the same. We do sometimes, for sure, but not as our go-to thing. Recall that the many different ways that LGBT people have discovered to have sex and get off are very much inspired by the AIDS crisis. Necessity is the mother of invention, and so we found ways to get hot with less "risky" activities. Some oral sex and some kink is enough to make most people happy.

This is the formula that has worked for me. I don't believe that it's a one-size-fits-all. However, I'm committed to safer sex and reducing risk while still enjoying my life.

There will be another deadly sexual infection that pops up eventually. That may not happen in my lifetime, but it certainly could. I still choose to go out, live my life, and have sex with new people without worrying constantly about STIs, rape, gay bashers, car crashes, public shootings, nuclear disaster, volcanic eruptions, or Donald Trump.

People I trusted told me the world was going to end in 2012. I worried. I "prepped" in a very different way. Instead of chaos and devastation, in 2012 we got PrEP and the rise of the new gender identity revolution. Shortly afterward, America received same-sex marriage and the rise of Black Lives Matter. Seems like we've been doing okay.

Eleven

Sage Your Asshole and Auld Lang Syne

30 tablets

℞ only

WHILE I WAS on winter holiday in Florida visiting my folks, I realized that I was running low on PrEP. *No worries*, I thought. *I can call it in now, fly back to Seattle on the 30th, and pick it up in time for New Year's Eve.* My new sex buddy Shaun and I had been texting and sexting while I was traveling, and it seemed very likely that we'd pick up where we left off and start hooking up more often when I got back, maybe even start dating.

I called my prescription in on the 29th, right on time. That way, I could pick it up on the 31st, respecting Group Health pharmacy's preferred two-day advance call-in. I even had an extra pill to last me through the first of January, 2016.

I flew back. I celebrated the New Year's Eve with Ylva, my best friend since FSU. We reveled with our witch friend Aubrey and a score of other weirdoes at the home of our friend Gayle, owner of a charming gothic curio and art store called Gargoyles Statuary. At midnight, Ylva and Aubrey and I sage-smudged our genitals front and back to refresh and cleanse them of old emotional baggage. Try it some time—your junk will smell kind of like barbecue for a day, but that can also be fun.

The next day, a Friday, I swallowed the last PrEP pill in my supply, I got dressed, and I walked a few blocks over to the pharmacy. There was lightness to my step on the first day of a new year. I thought about seeing Shaun again. I thought about how I'd write the book you're reading.

As I rounded the corner of the Group Health parking lot, I saw it completely empty of cars. You probably know the feeling—you've made a trip to get something, something you need that very day, like your PrEP refill or toilet paper or tampons. You get there and the parking lot is empty but for a motley crew of squirrels and crows chomping nervously on a few bacon-ranch Corn Nuts from a spilled baggie.

I walked up to the glass doors, just in case I was wrong, or perhaps I could through sheer force of will make them open magically on this national holiday. Maybe I should've saged my package a bit more thoroughly. The squirrels and the crows mocked me quietly.

As if to add insult to thirstiness, the hours of operation were clearly displayed on the doors: *closed on Saturday and Sunday*—the following two days. Mother fuck. That meant I would have to reorder it and drive across town to the open-late emergency pharmacy, but that's not why I have Facebook. I have Facebook so that I can crowdsource anything. I put out a hivemind bulletin.

I received immediate offers. People were eager to share and keep me safely on my regimen. Swope texted me to say he'd give me whatever I needed if I would meet him out on the town that night.

I never thought I'd get so attached to PrEP, but it makes sense in hindsight. If I stopped taking PrEP now, or I couldn't afford it, would my HIV fears creep back?

As you might expect, the protection that PrEP offers decreases day by day as long as you're not taking it. I'm not sure of the percentage decrease of protection vs. the days without taking the pill, divided by the X-axis of blood tests and square to the Y-axis of barebacking with a train of Brooklyn hipsters at a loft orgy.

There are the important reasons to be careful *how* and *why* you stop using PrEP, but none of them are reasons to stay on the drug indefinitely. For the near-universal majority of us who are on PrEP and do not have HIV or hepatitis B, we can literally just stop taking it altogether. Unlike other drugs that require weaning to avoid some side effects, an abrupt discontinuation of PrEP use is safe if other circumstances are appropriately in line. I wasn't ready to have a PrEP interruption. It was a new year, and Shaun awaited my tender bonking.

I picked Swope up from a club called Kremwerk later that night. He was out and about as Heavy Scene Macaque, which meant he was now seven feet tall in a day-glow catsuit and a vibrant wig in two unnatural colors, like a two-flavor snow cone. There's something of Katy Perry in Heavy's looks, but there's also something of Oopsy the Clown, and Swope will be the first, last, and median person to admit this.

Heavy and their entourage were just leaving Kremwerk. Heavy stooped to get their fourteen-inch broken mirror tiara through the doorway. Heavy Scene Macaque goes hard.

We rendezvoused on the street, as though Heavy were my dealer. "Yo queen," they said. "I hear you need your PrEP fix."

I tried to hug Heavy, but when they're all dolled up, it's like trying to hug a mannequin without knocking it over. They pulled out their bottle of PrEP and said I could have as much as I needed.

Heavy, or rather Swope, has always been a very generous and supportive friend. Swope's heart is loyal, forgiving, and charitable. I've never seen him stay mad at anyone, even those who've done the worst to him. I used to be in love with him. Who wouldn't be?

I took three pills and stowed them in the watch pocket of my jeans. Yes, that fifth pocket was created for a watch—*The More You Know*. I wrangled Heavy's entourage into my car and dropped them off at Denny and Broadway, then I went home. I needed my health and beauty rest.

A few days later, we went out to Araya's Thai for their lunch buffet, and I gave Swope back three little blue Truvada pills. We talked about our dating and sex lives, per the usual. I talked about Shaun and his interesting quirks and how he's a much hotter weirdo than I'd first expected. Swope told me about old boyfriends who wouldn't stay dead. In between stuffing my face with crispy spring rolls and sweet black rice pudding, I quipped, "So yeah, at this point, I'll pretty much hook up with anyone I'm attracted to, as long as he isn't a jerk."

Did I really just say that? I thought later about how deeply that statement runs. Anyone—as long as I feel attracted and he treats me with dignity and kindness. Those are some bottom-line requirements I learned the hard way.

Had I, former virgin college freshman, former prude, sexual assault survivor, formerly afraid to the core of what HIV might do to me—had I really just said in casual, confident honesty that I'd have sex with anyone I like? I meant it.

Damn. I've come pretty far.

THE PERSONAL EFFECTS of PrEP continue for me. I still haven't had a single negative physical side effect, and I've been on it since August 2014. I meet guys all the time who report that they have a lot of stomach discomfort during the first month. I'm sure that's a deterrent for some, but I've never heard from anyone who stopped taking PrEP just because he had some stomach issues in the first weeks. We joke about it—*of course you're not going to contract HIV while on PrEP! You're too sick to your stomach to fuck.*

I'm so glad that the jellyfish and centipedes and squid that live among my gut flora didn't flip out when I started taking it. I do not look forward to the gallons of kombucha that I as a white person am expected to drink any time I have an upset stomach.

I love PrEP. I love it, love it, love it. It allows me to go into each new dating or sexual situation with absolutely no fears about HIV. I grew up terrified of AIDS. I grew up afraid that I'd get it from love, from rape, from a hasty blowjob between strangers. I grew into manhood terrified of AIDS. Now that I'm in my thirties and PrEP is real and poz-undetectable status is real, I'm giddy to have all the friendly, informed, affectionate sex I missed out on as a younger man.

I'm not avoiding a committed relationship, nor am I avoiding monogamy. I desire both of these things. I'd like to have a husband and some children (yeah, I guess I want a family). I'm just genderqueer and kinky enough that I get really excited by the idea of my partner and me roleplaying that we're getting each other pregnant. However, none of this has happened, and I have fewer and fewer qualms about opening Grindr or Scruff on my phone and setting up a date. I still prefer to meet people in person, but dammit, I have a book to write. Opening the online menu and ordering a man-pizza is just too convenient right now.

Writing this book has required that I face quite a few fears. I was afraid that I'd spend a year on it, pour my soul into it, tell the world my most intimate business, and then no one would notice it. Or worse: what if the world did notice it, and people hated it, calling me a literary exhibitionist who can't resist telling everyone about the graphic details of my sex life? What if the reviews come back and they're miserable? What if I die alone and penniless, and my greyhound eats my face before they find me, and I have to have a closed casket funeral?!

Calm the hell down, Evan J. Peterson. It's just a book. It's just a bunch of words. What people say and write about you is also just a bunch of words.

I thought this book would be an excellent occasion to finally learn how to bottom. Just as I don't want to miss out on sex in general, I don't want to miss out on this kind of sex that has been so daunting to me my whole life. I want to try everything in life, as long as it doesn't sound like a horrible idea. Bottoming? Boy, howdy! Getting choked until I pass out while I orgasm? No, thank you, but have a safe and sane good time if that's your thing.

The fear of AIDS certainly had powerful sway over my avoidance of bottoming. I've enjoyed occasional attention to my ass, but when it comes to inviting a cock in, it's been a lifelong difficulty to get past the fear of HIV, the fear of pain, the fear of being that vulnerable to someone.

Several friends offered to deflower me. One poz-undetectable former lover said he'd do it, but he insists on condomless sex. I'm glad I didn't take him up on the offer; he tested positive for syphilis a few months later. A while after that, his boyfriend (HIV-negative and on PrEP, for the record) also offered to do the deed. That man is someone for whom I have much affection, but it's not sexual. I wasn't going to spend my last remaining V-card on awkward sex.

While writing this book, I spent a lot of time with my friend Alex, who writes fantasy novels. We'd get together to write and edit. I've always had an enormous crush on him. I know Alex isn't interested in a romantic relationship with me, nor a merely sexual one. But.

I'd been feeling very connected with him at that time; he knew I was looking for someone to help me clear the bottoming hurdle. For the book, of course. What a tidy resolution: after a decade and a half of adulthood, I finally get up the resolve and confidence to bottom. Thanks, Truvada!

Alex fit what I was looking for perfectly: a trusted friend, someone who is attentive to his sexual partners, and a man that I'm very attracted to. I would do pretty much anything in bed with Alex. Also, I felt sure that it wouldn't disrupt our friendship if I asked him, regardless of his answer.

I sprang the question on him via text. I figured that wouldn't change his answer, and it gave me the confidence to do it without creating an awkward in-person situation. I'm no saint about confidence and direct communication.

> **EJP:**   *Hey you. Do you have a few minutes to talk?*

> **Alex:**   *Sure. Everything okay?*

> **EJP:**   *Yeah, everything's great. I just want to have a serious conversation with you.*

> **Alex:**   *Okay. Shoot.*

> **EJP:**   *I've put a lot of thought into this. I know this has never been on the table in the past, but would you like to be the first person to top me?*

That was worth a shot, right? I know a dozen guys who would've said, *OMG yes can we do that tonight?* Alex answered quickly and perfectly: *Thank you, but that's not where I see our friendship going.*

Dammit, Alex. You're even perfect when you're turning me down.

So we went back to writing and editing together. C'est la vie en rose. I reflected for a while on my motivations for getting fucked in the butt. At bottom, no pun intended, I want to open my body up and try new things. PrEP has indeed helped me be ready for that, but so has therapy, twelve-step recovery, and being surrounded by experienced (really goddamn experienced) bottoms, many of whom are also tops. But is it really that important? I love the sex I have now, most of the time. I love the men I get to have it with.

I finally came to the conclusion that this book is complete without a torrid account of me discovering the joys of getting pounded. I have no convincing reason to force myself into doing anything sexual just so I'll have something to write about. Forcing myself to have sex sounds a lot like sexually assaulting myself. I have plenty to write about without troubling those waters.

For fuck's sake, Evan J. Peterson. Save something for the sequel.

The
PrEPilogue

30 tablets

R̞ only

So MANY THINGS have happened, and continue to happen, since I began writing this book. For one thing, Donald Trump has been elected President of the United States. Heaven knows if he'll even take office, since he never thought he would be elected, and I doubt he wants this job.

We have no idea what will become of the Affordable Care Act and the new access it has created to HIV medications, including PrEP. Trump and his Republican-dominated Congress have vowed to dismantle the ACA, even though the U.S. Supreme Court has already had its say on the matter. As I write this, minutes ago, I received a message from a close friend, an MD who teaches as well as practices, about organizing to tell Congress to keep Obamacare.

Trump's Vice President, Mike Pence[6], has a dismal reputation on LGBTQ issues, not to mention HIV issues. Pence did approve a needle-exchange program in Indiana during a surge in HIV infections, after a Congressional record of opposing funding such measures[7], so he isn't completely beyond a change of heart (after intense prayer, of course).

In October 2015, Scruff (still my favorite dating app) rolled out new profile options that allow users to flag what kind of sex they like (top, bottom, oral, no sex, etc.) as well as their prevention methods (PrEP, condoms, etc.). This shows how widespread and normal PrEP use has become in gay populations—at least in countries in which the drug is available and affordable.

The following June, seemingly immediately after winning *RuPaul's Drag Race* and becoming America's new gay superstar, Bob the Drag Queen starred in a ferocious yet educational PSA video for the *#HIVBeats* project[8] and *Greater than AIDS* non-profit (a collaboration between the Black AIDS Institute and the Kaiser Family Foundation). Bob, who may be even funnier and more charismatic than Bianca Del Rio (sorry, Roy), flounces around with backup dancers and nearly licks his lips when saying, "Pre-Exposure Prophylaxis." Bob, if you're reading this, call me.

Right after I signed my book deal contract, PrEP was famously featured for the first time on TV. On the ABC show *How to Get Away With Murder*, a serodiscordant gay couple talked it over. On television!

Still, I meet people every day in America who aren't familiar with PrEP: nurses. Pharmacists. In fact it seems like I meet more heterosexual science journalists and science fiction authors who are aware of PrEP than medical workers who are familiar. How is that possible?

Meanwhile, outside of the civilized world, the United Kingdom's National Health Service is in a long battle with its own citizens (and courts) over whether making PrEP available to the public is worth it. An article in *The Guardian*[9] states that about four thousand people in the UK contract HIV every year. That number of new infections should give anyone pause; considering the amount it costs to treat HIV in a single individual, it's cost effective and humane to fund prevention. According to the article, it costs 360,000 British pounds to treat HIV infection over a lifetime.

In a country with socialized health care, they're fighting over whether the government should fund a drug that's virtually 100% effective at prevention. Apparently, they'd rather be spending the money on managing infections. It's no surprise that a huge part of the UK Leave campaign (to exit the European Union) was the panicked talk about so many immigrants choking citizens out of available doctor's services. That's more than just anti-Muslim racism, by the way;

according to trusted British friends, a large part of the resented UK immigrant population is white continental Europeans such as the Polish. We in the US have been having that same argument over other social services, so don't be surprised when it pops up in regard to government assistance with PrEP.

Australia is also enduring its own bureaucratic blocks to PrEP. In May 2016, their government's Therapeutic Goods Association (TGA) approved Truvada to be used as PrEP (Truvada had already been available for HIV-positive citizens). The next step will be to make Truvada's use as PrEP affordable as part of their "pharmaceutical benefits scheme," or PBS[10]. Oh, those government acronyms. According to an article at abc.net.au[11], many Australians have been getting their PrEP through clinical trials, international drug shipments, or the ever-reliable black market. PrEP is so sought-after that people are buying and selling it on the black market, like recreational drugs or human organs.

Gallows humor aside, people are desperate enough for PrEP that they're buying it illegally. *That* is the power of effective prevention. These are the lengths to which people will go to feel safe.

As of March 2016, only six countries—six freakin' countries in the whole world—had approved PrEP for regulated use: the United States, France, Canada, Israel, Kenya, and South Africa. You read that correctly; Kenya has had available PrEP while Australia, the UK, Mexico, the EU, Brazil, Thailand, China, Japan, India, etc., were or are still catching up. South Africa has a government that in the twenty-first-fucking-century officially denied that HIV is connected to AIDS (and as a result let 300,000 people die[12]—oopsy daisy!). Now, South Africa has PrEP while most of the world does not.

I'm in a polite (for Twitter) debate with someone who is attempting to grill me about the public funding of PrEP in the UK. I'm not sure who I'm talking to; the pic is an ad (for what, it isn't clear), and the person on the other end is likely a UK resident, but anything's possible in Twitterland.

They're asking me if I've considered the economic costs of making PrEP available through the NHS. They ask such mind-blowing questions as, "If I drive dangerously and refuse to wear a seatbelt, will [the NHS] fund me a crash helmet?" and the ever-vague, "Would #PrEP be easier on society?" I'm not sure what is meant by "easier" or "society."

In rebuttal, I've asked them, "Which costs more: treatment or prevention?" Eventually I decided the best way to de-escalate would be to invite them to the US to have condomless sex while on Truvada.

They declined! Can you believe that shit? Anyway, I was able to get the last word while also being polite and encouraging that they read up on PrEP's success in Canada and the US. The manchild in me always wants to have the last word on social media, and this is something I need to get over in time for the publication of this book.

@evanjpeterson, just sayin'.

In 2017, people are still resisting PrEP as prevention. People think condoms should be "enough." Don't forget all the millions of people who think that those homosexuals should just clean up their acts, and that anyone who contracts HIV probably deserved it for having the "wrong" kind of sex.

I've heard this argument here in the US. It's the same old same old. People don't want their tax dollars to fund obese people's health care (spoiler: your tax dollars already do, and they did so long before Obamacare). They don't want their taxes to fund HIV care *or* prevention (ditto). Consider all of the safe sex, anti-smoking, "Just Say No to Drugs," and healthy eating campaigns you've seen on television and on ads. Who do you think is paying for those prevention messages?

Condoms aren't "enough." They're a very useful form of prevention, but they've never been "enough." No amount of wishing and hoping and "should" is going to change that. People are going to have sex. They're going to have it without condoms. People—straight, queer, no matter—have been having condomless sex for thirty years of the AIDS epidemic, and thousands of years before that.

Sex is a human right, just like food and water. We have as much right to have healthy sex as we do to affordable food and clean water. Right now, in 2017, healthy sex means making PrEP available to those who are at risk. Condoms do work, but they haven't erased the disease. Not in America, not in Africa, not anywhere else.

Previous years' arguments claimed that PrEP is only moderately effective if taken daily, and then only when paired with condoms and other prevention factors. There were charming little charts and graphics released by certain AIDS organizations to disparage PrEP's effectiveness. This led to accusations from the gay and poz communities that such organizations are in the business of treating HIV infections, not preventing them. You may recall that the CEO of the AIDS Healthcare Foundation referred to PrEP as a "party drug," as though it were crystal meth. Except it can't get you high, or I'd be zonked every day on that stuff.

They're wrong. PrEP has been remarkably effective. As I go through my final edits of this book, out of the thousands upon thousands of people on PrEP (estimated forty thousand in the US alone), there have been only three reported cases of HIV infection while someone was taking daily doses.

Three. That's more than moderately effective. In fact, it's more than the popularly quoted "99% effective." It's closer to 99.999% effective. These patients are the exception that proves the rule, and I'll take those odds just to feel confident and relaxed about sex.

In March 2016, media sources began to report the story of "Joe," the first person on record to contract HIV while taking PrEP religiously. He's been interviewed anonymously by *POZ* magazine[13], and to hear him tell it, he isn't mad at PrEP or Gilead Sciences. I tried to contact him through the *POZ* staff, but as of this writing, he has not responded.

Here are the facts: he was having sex with partners who were known to be HIV-positive and undetectable, which (as I've said over and over) is a very reliable way to stay HIV-negative. He decided to hook up with someone who believed they were HIV-negative, but they weren't. They had a rare strain of HIV that happened to be resistant to the two drugs that come in a Truvada pill (emtricitabine and tenofovir). Even so, the quarterly HIV tests that are required for PrEP users caught his infection early, and he went on HIV meds that worked on his strain of the virus. His viral load became quickly undetectable.

He doesn't resent PrEP. He doesn't resent the man who gave him HIV. He doesn't seem to resent himself, either. I wish we were all more like that guy.

Acknowledgments

FIRSTLY, THANKS TO the men who brought me to the party: To Steve Berman, thank you for believing in the potential of PrEP, and for believing that I am the one to write this book for Lethe Press. To Christopher Frizzelle, thank you for choosing me to write about this amazing breakthrough in *The Stranger*. Thanks to Mathew Rodriguez and JD Davids, my editors at TheBody.com.

Thanks to the queers whose books and essays taught me how to write compelling nonfiction and humor: Kate Bornstein, James St. James, Jayne County, Samuel R. Delany, William S. Burroughs, Truman Capote, Alison Bechdel, Augusten Burroughs, David Sedaris, David Schmader, and Dan Savage. To the straight essayists as well: Angela Carter, Stephen King, Leonard Pitts, Jr., Carl Hiassen, and Dave Barry.

To everyone who taught me how to read and write—Mom and Dad, Danielle, Pat Roberts, all of the elementary and middle school teachers (even Mrs. Hoolihan and Mrs. Braun who were scabrous harpies to me), high school teachers like Patrick Scaffetti, Patricia Manley, Loretta Pinder, Kecia McAlpine, Lorraine Liverpool, and Delania Cunningham, and the college mentors: David Kirby, Diane Roberts, Ginny Grimsley, Barbara Hamby, Ken Foster, Erin Belieu, Robert Olen Butler, Deborah Coxwell Teague, and Ormond Loomis. Extra special thanks to the Clarion West mentors Andy Duncan, Eileen Gunn, Toby Buckell, Susan Palwick, Nalo Hopkinson, and Cory Doctorow. Thanks as well to Neile Graham, Huw Evans, and Nisi Shawl for inviting me into the Clarion West family.

Thanks to my Clarion West siblings and cousins who gave so much encouragement during this process: Tegan Moore, Julia Wetherell, Nibs Sen, Mimi Mondal, Laurie Penney, Margaret Killjoy, Leo Vladimirsky, Rebecca Campbell, Thersa Matsuura, Justin Key, Christine Neulieb, Mike Sebastian, Jake Stone, Garret Johnson, Nana Nkweti,

Dinesh Pulandram, Sam Kolawole, Betsy Aoki, Paul DesCombaz, Liz Argle, Scott James Magner, Karen Gussoff, Vicki Saunders, Caroline Bobanick, Caroline Yoachim, Tod McCoy, Lauren Dixon, Katie Sparrow, and on and on.

Thanks to my beta readers: Javier X, Gwen Cho, Betsy Aoki, Jim Swenson, Amy Shepherd, Tegan Moore, Joe Brock and Kent Rogers.

Thanks to my media and PR coaching and Wikipedia team: Garret Johnston, Lane Rasberry, and Kyle Ankney.

Thanks to Matt Bright for cover design and for laying me this book out.

Thanks to my whole family for endless love and support, even when we're mad at each other. I hope you don't get too terribly embarrassed reading this book.

AND TO THE somewhere between seventy and eighty dudes I've hooked up with so far: Y'all are wonderful and lovable—except the very few of you who are lovable but also cruel and destructive messes. Let's all do better.

Endnotes

[1] Peterson, Evan J. "The Case for PrEP, or How I Learned to Stop Worrying and Love HIV-Positive Guys." *TheStranger.com*. Nov. 12, 2014

[2] Gorman, Anna & Alexandra Zavis. "Christine Maggiore, vocal skeptic of AIDS research, dies at 52." *LATimes.com*. Dec. 30, 2008

[3] Kalichman, Seth. "HIV, AIDS, and One Year Later: No Rest for Christine Maggiore." *Denyingaids.blogspot.com*. Dec. 11, 2009

[4] Teeter, Tim. "HIV Causes AIDS: Proof Derived from Koch's Postulates." *TheBody.com*. 2000.

[5] Peterson, Evan J. "PrEP: So Effective, It's Unheard Of." *TheBody.com*. Feb. 27, 2015.

[6] Nichols, Chris. "True: Mike Pence advocated for 'conversion therapy.'" *Politifact.com*. Jul. 28, 2016.

[7] Twohey, Megan. "Mike Pence's Response to H. I. V. Outbreak: Prayer, Then a Change of Heart." *NYTimes.com*. Aug. 7, 2016.

[8] Bob the Drag Queen. "'Oh Hey! Prepare Yourself!' by Bob the Drag Queen for #HIVBEATS." *YouTube.com*. Jun. 5, 2016.

[9] Bosely, Sarah. "NHS can fund 'game-changing' PrEP HIV drug, court says" *TheGuardian.com*. Aug 2, 2016.

[10] AFAO. "AFAO Welcomes Approval of Truvada for PrEP." *Australian Federation of AIDS Organizations. AFAO.org.au*. May 6, 2016.

[11] McCormack, Ange. "'Groundbreaking" HIV prevention pill approved by TGA in Australia." *Australian Broadcasting Organization. ABC.net.au*. May 6, 2016.

[12] Harvard School of Public Health. "Researchers estimate lives lost due to delay in antiretroviral drug use for HIV/AIDS in South Africa." *HSPH.harvard.edu*. Oct. 20, 2008.

[13] Straube, Trenton. "Meet the Man Who Got HIV While on Daily PrEP." *POZ.com*. Mar. 3, 2016.

CPSIA information can be obtained
at www.ICGtesting.com
Printed in the USA
FSOW02n2352220417
33364FS

9 781590 215791